LECTURES ON LANGUAGE.

As Particularly Connected With English Grammar

- William Stevens Balch -

LECTURE I.

GENERAL VIEW OF LANGUAGE.

Study of Language long considered difficult. — Its importance. — Errors in teaching. — Not understood by Teachers. — Attachment to old systems. — Improvement preferable. — The subject important. — Its advantages. — Principles laid down. — Orthography. — Etymology. — Syntax. — Prosody.

LADIES AND GENTLEMEN,

It is proposed to commence, this evening, a course of Lectures on the Grammar of the English Language. I am aware of the difficulties attending this subject, occasioned not so much by any fault in itself, as by the thousand and one methods adopted to teach it, the multiplicity of books pretending to "simplify" it, and the vast contrariety of opinion entertained by those who profess to be its masters. By many it has been considered a needless affair, an unnecessary appendage to a common education; by others, altogether beyond the reach of common capacities; and by all, cold, lifeless, and uninteresting, full of doubts and perplexities, where the wisest have differed, and the firmest often changed opinions.

All this difficulty originates, I apprehend, in the wrong view that is taken of the subject. The most beautiful landscape may appear at great disadvantage, if viewed from an unfavorable position. I would be slow to believe that the means on which depends the whole business of the community, the study of the sciences, all improvement upon the past, the history of all nations in all ages of the world, social intercourse, oral or written, and, in a great measure, the knowledge of God, and the hopes of immortality, can be either unworthy of study, or, if rightly explained, uninteresting in the acquisition. In fact, on the principles I am about to advocate, I have seen the deepest interest manifested, from the small child to the grey-headed sire, from the mere novice to the statesman and philosopher, and all alike seemed to be edified and improved by the attention bestowed upon the subject.

I confess, however, that with the mention of *grammar*, an association of ideas are called up by no means agreeable. The mind involuntarily reverts to the days of childhood, when we were compelled, at the risk of our bodily safety, to commit to memory a set of arbitrary rules, which we could neither understand nor apply in the correct use of language. Formerly it was never dreamed that grammar depended on any higher authority than the books put into our hands. And learners were not only dissuaded, but strictly forbidden to go beyond the limits set them in the etymological and syntactical rules of the authors to whom they were referred. If a query ever arose in their minds, and they modestly proposed a plain question as to the *why* and *wherefore* things were thus, instead of giving an answer according to common sense, in a way to be understood, the authorities were pondered over, till some rule or remark could be found which would apply, and this settled the matter with "proof as strong as holy writ." In this way an end may be put to the inquiry; but the thinking mind will hardly be satisfied with the mere opinion of another, who has no evidence to afford, save the undisputed dignity of his station, or the authority of books. This course is easily accounted for. Rather than expose his own ignorance, the teacher quotes the printed ignorance of others, thinking, no doubt, that folly and nonsense will appear better second-handed, than fresh from his own responsibility. Or else on the more common score, that "misery loves company."

Teachers have not unfrequently found themselves placed in an unenviable position by the honest inquiries of some thinking urchin, who has demanded why "*one noun governs* another in the possessive case," as "master's slave;" why there are more tenses than *three*; what is meant by a *neuter* verb, which "signifies neither action nor passion;" or an "intransitive verb," which expresses the highest possible action, but terminates on no object; a cause without an effect; why *that* is sometimes a pronoun, sometimes an adjective, and not unfrequently a conjunction, &c. &c. They may have succeeded, by dint of official authority, in silencing such inquiries, but they have failed to give a satisfactory answer to the questions proposed.

Long received opinions may, in some cases, become law, pleading no other reason than antiquity. But this is an age of investigation, which demands the most lucid and unequivocal proof of the point assumed. The dogmatism of the schoolmen will no longer satisfy. The dark ages of mental servility are passing away. The day light of science has long since dawned upon the world, and the noon day of truth, reason, and virtue, will ere long be established on a firm and immutable basis. The human mind, left free to investigate, will gradually advance onward in the course of knowledge and goodness marked out by the Creator, till it attains to that perfection which shall constitute its highest glory, its truest bliss.

You will perceive, at once, that our inquiries thro out these lectures will not be bounded by what has been said or written on the subject. We take a wider range. We adopt no sentiment because it is ancient or popular. We refer to no authority but what proves itself to be correct. And we ask no one to adopt our opinions any farther than they agree with the fixed laws of nature in the regulation of matter and thought, and apply in common practice among men.

Have we not a right to expect, in return, that you will be equally honest to yourselves and the subject before us? So far as the errors of existing systems shall be exposed, will you not reject them, and adopt whatever appears conclusively true and practically useful? Will you, can you, be satisfied to adopt for yourselves and teach to others, systems of grammar, for no other reason than because they are old, and claim the support of the learned and honorable?

Such a course, generally adopted, would give the ever-lasting quietus to all improvement. It would be a practical adoption of the philosophy of the Dutchman, who was content to carry his grist in one end of the sack and a stone to balance it in the other, assigning for a reason, that his honored father had always done so before him. Who would be content to adopt the astrology of the ancients, in preferance to astronomy as now taught, because the latter is more modern? Who would spend three years in transcribing a copy of the Bible, when a better could be obtained for one dollar, because manuscripts were thus procured in former times? What lady would prefer to take her cards, wheel, and loom, and spend a month or two in manufacturing for herself a dress, when a better could be earned in half the time, merely because her respected grandmother did so before her? Who would go back a thousand years to find a model for society, rejecting all improvements in the arts and sciences, because they are innovations, encroachments upon the opinions and practices of learned and honorable men?

I can not believe there is a person in this respected audience whose mind is in such voluntary slavery as to induce the adoption of such a course. I see before me minds which sparkle in every look, and thoughts which are ever active, to acquire what is true, and adopt what is useful. And I flatter myself that the time spent in the investigation of the science of language will not be unpleasant or unprofitable.

I feel the greater confidence from the consideration that your minds are yet untrammeled; not but what many, probably most of you, have already studied the popular systems of grammar, and understood them; if such a thing is possible; but because you have shown a disposition to learn, by becoming members of this Institute, the object of which is the improvement of its members.

Let us therefore make an humble attempt, with all due candor and discretion, to enter upon the inquiry before us with an unflinching determination to push our investigations beyond all reasonable doubt, and never rest satisfied till we have conquered all conquerable obstacles, and come into the possession of the light and liberty of truth.

The attempt here made will not be considered unimportant, by those who have known the difficulties attending the study of language. If any course can be marked out to shorten the time tediously spent in the acquisition of what is rarely attained—a thoro knowledge of language—a great benefit will result to the community; children will save months and years to engage in other useful attainments, and the high aspirations of the mind for truth and knowledge will not be curbed in its first efforts to improve by a set of technical and arbitrary rules. They will acquire a habit of thinking, of deep reflection; and never adopt, for fact, what appears unreasonable or inconsistent, merely because great or good men have said it is so. They will feel an independence of their own, and adopt a course of investigation which cannot fail of the most important consequences. It is not the saving of time, however, for which we propose a change in the system of teaching language. In this respect, it is the study of one's life. New facts are constantly developing themselves, new combinations of ideas and words are discovered, and new beauties presented at every advancing step. It is to acquire a knowledge of correct principles, to induce a habit of correct thinking, a freedom of investigation, and at that age when the character and language of life are forming. It is, in short, to exhibit before you truth of the greatest practical importance, not only to you, but to generations yet unborn, in the most essential affairs of human life, that I have broached the hated subject of grammar, and undertaken to reflect light upon this hitherto dark and disagreeable subject.

With a brief sketch of the outlines of language, as based on the fixed laws of nature, and the agreement of those who employ it, I shall conclude the present lecture.

We shall consider all language as governed by the invariable laws of nature, and as depending on the conventional regulations of men.

Words are the signs of ideas. Ideas are the impressions of things. Hence, in all our attempts to investigate the important principles of language, we shall employ the sign as the means of coming at the thing signified.

Language has usually been considered under four divisions, viz.: Orthography, Etymology, Syntax, and Prosody.

Orthography is *right spelling*; the combination of certain letters into words in such a manner as to agree with the spoken words used to denote an idea. We shall not labor this point, altho we conceive a great improvement might be effected in this department of learning. My only wish is to select from all the forms of spelling, the most simple and consistent. Constant changes are taking place in the method of making words, and we would not refuse to cast in our mite to make the standard more correct and easy. We would prune off by degrees all unnecessary appendages, as unsounded or italic letters, and write out words so as to be capable of a distinct pronunciation. But this change must be *gradually* effected. From the spelling adopted two centuries ago, a wonderful improvement has taken place. And we have not yet gone beyond the possibility of improvement. Let us not be too sensitive on this point, nor too tenacious of old forms. Most of our dictionaries differ in many respects in regard to the true system of orthography, and our true course is to adopt every improvement which is offered. Thro out this work we shall spell some words different from what is customary, but intend not, thereby, to incur the ignominy of bad spellers. Let small improvements be adopted, and our language may soon be redeemed from the difficulties which have perplexed beginners in their first attempts to convey ideas by written words.[1]

In that department of language denominated Etymology, we shall contend that all words are reducible to two general classes, nouns and verbs; or, *things* and *actions*. We shall, however, admit of subdivisions, and treat of pronouns, adjectives, and contractions. We shall contend for only two cases of nouns, one kind of pronouns, one kind of verbs, that all are active; three modes, and as many tenses; that articles, adverbs, prepositions, conjunctions, and interjections, have no distinctive character, no existence, in fact, to warrant a "local habitation or a name."

In the composition of sentences, a few general rules of Syntax may be given; but the principal object to be obtained, is the possession of correct ideas derived from a knowledge of things, and the most approved words to express them; the combination of words in a sentence will readily enough follow.

Prosody relates to the quantity of syllables, rules of accent and pronunciation, and the arrangement of syllables and words so as to produce harmony. It applies specially to versification. As our object is not to make poets, who, it is said, "are born, and not made," but to teach the true principles of language, we shall give no attention to this finishing stroke of composition.

In our next we shall lay before you the principles upon which all language depends, and the process by which its use is to be acquired.

LECTURE II.

FUNDAMENTAL PRINCIPLES OF LANGUAGE.

General principles of Language. — Business of Grammar. — Children are Philosophers. — Things, ideas, and words. — Actions. — Qualities of things. — Words without ideas. — Grammatical terms inappropriate. — Principles of Language permanent. — Errors in mental science. — Facts admit of no change. — Complex ideas. — Ideas of qualities. — An example. — New ideas. — Unknown words. — Signs without things signified. — Fixed laws regulate matter and mind.

All language depends on two general principles.

First. The fixed and unvarying laws of nature which regulate matter and mind.

Second. The agreement of those who use it.

In accordance with these principles all language must be explained. It is not only needless but impossible for us to deviate from them. They remain the same in all ages and in all countries. It should be the object of the grammarian, and of all who employ language in the expression of ideas, to become intimately acquainted with their use.

It is the business of grammar to explain, not only verbal language, but also the sublime principles upon which all written or spoken language depends. It forms an important part of physical and mental science, which, correctly explained, is abundantly simple and extensively useful in its application to the affairs of human life and the promotion of human enjoyment.

It will not be contended that we are assuming a position beyond the capacities of learners, that the course here adopted is too philosophic. Such is not the fact. Children are philosophers by nature. All their ideas are derived from things as presented to their observations. No mother learns her child to lisp the name of a thing which has no being, but she chooses objects with which it is most familiar, and which are most constantly before it; such as father, mother, brother, sister.

She constantly points to the object named, that a distinct impression may be made upon its mind, and the thing signified, the idea of the thing, and the name which represents it, are all inseparably associated together. If the father is absent, the child may *think* of him from the idea or impression which his person and affection has produced in the mind. If the mother pronounces his *name* with which it has become familiar, the child will start, look about for the object, or thing signified by the *name*, father, and not being able to discover him, will settle down contented with the *idea* of him deeply impressed on the mind, and as distinctly understood as if the father was present in person. So with every thing else.

Again, after the child has become familiar with the name of the being called father; the name, idea and object itself being intimately associated the mother will next begin to teach it another lesson; following most undeviatingly the course which nature and true philosophy mark out. The father comes and goes, is present or absent. She says on his return, father *come*, and the little one looks round to see the thing signified by the word father, the idea of which is distinctly impressed on the mind, and which it now sees present before it. But this loved object has not always been here. It had looked round and called for the father. But the mother had told it *he was gone*. Father gone, father come, is her language, and here the child begins to learn ideas of actions. Of this it had, at first, no notion whatever, and never thought of the father except when his person was present before it, for no impressions had been distinctly made upon the mind which could be called up by a sound of which it could have no conceptions whatever. Now that it has advanced so far, the idea of the father is retained, even tho he is himself absent, and the child begins to associate the notion of coming and going with his presence or absence. Following out this course the mind becomes acquainted with things and actions, or the changes which things undergo.

Next, the mother begins to learn her offspring the distinction and qualities of things. When the little sister comes to it in innocent playfulness the mother says, "*good* sister," and with the descriptive word *good* it soon begins to associate the quality expressed by the affectionate regard, of its sister. But when that sister strikes the child, or pesters it in any way, the mother says "*naughty* sister," "bad sister." It soon comprehends the descriptive words, *good* and *bad*, and along with them carries the association of ideas which such conduct produces. In the same way it learns to distinguish the difference between *great* and *small*, *cold* and *hot*, hard and soft.

In this manner the child becomes acquainted with the use of language. It first becomes acquainted with things, the idea of which is left upon the mind, or, more properly, the *impression of which*, left on the mind, *constitutes the idea*; and a vocabulary of words are learned, which represent these ideas, from which it may select those best calculated to express its meaning whenever a conversation is had with another.

You will readily perceive the correctness of our first proposition, that all language depends on the fixed and unerring laws of nature. Things exist. A knowledge of them produces ideas in the mind, and sounds or signs are adopted as vehicles to convey these ideas from one to another.

It would be absurd and ridiculous to suppose that any person, however great, or learned, or wise, could employ language correctly without a knowledge of the things expressed by that language. No matter how chaste his words, how lofty his phrases, how sweet the intonations, or mellow the accents. It would avail him nothing if *ideas* were not represented thereby. It would all be an unknown tongue to the hearer or reader. It would not be like the loud rolling thunder, for that tells the wondrous power of God. It would not be like the soft zephyrs of evening, the radiance of the sun, the twinkling of the stars; for they speak the intelligible language of sublimity itself, and tell of the kindness and protection of our Father who is in heaven. It would not be like the sweet notes of the choral songsters of the grove, for they warble hymns of gratitude to God; not like the boding of the distant owl, for that tells the profound solemnity of night; not like the hungry lion roaring for his prey, for that tells of death and plunder; not like the distant notes of the clarion, for that tells of blood and carnage, of tears and anguish, of widowhood and orphanage. It can be compared to nothing but a Babel of confusion in which their own folly is worse confounded. And yet, I am sorry to say it, the languages of all ages and nations have been too frequently perverted, and compiled into a heterogeneous mass of abstruse, metaphysical volumes, whose only recommendation is the elegant bindings in which they are enclosed.

And grammars themselves, whose pretended object is to teach the rules of speaking and writing correctly, form but a miserable exception to this sweeping remark. I defy any grammarian, author, or teacher of the numberless systems, which come, like the frogs of Egypt, all of one genus, to cover the land, to give a reasonable explanation of even the terms they employ to define their meaning, if indeed, meaning they have. What is meant by an "*in*-definite article," a *dis*-junctive *con*-junction, an *ad*-verb which qualifies an *adjective*, and "sometimes another *ad*-verb?" Such "parts of speech" have no existence in fact, and their adoption in rules of grammar, have been found exceedingly mischievous and perplexing. "Adverbs and conjunctions," and "*adverbial* phrases," and "conjunctive expressions," may serve as common sewers for a large and most useful class of words, which the teachers of grammar and lexicographers have been unable to explain; but learners will gain little information by being told that such is an *adverbial phrase*, and such, a *conjunctive expression*. This is an easy method, I confess, a sort of wholesale traffic, in parsing (*passing*) language, and may serve to cloak the ignorance of the teachers and makers of grammars. But it will reflect little light on the principles of language, or prove very efficient helps to "speak or write with propriety." Those who *think*, will demand the *meaning* of these words, and the reason of their use. When that is ascertained, little difficulty will be found in giving them a place in the company of respectable words. But I am digressing. More shall be said upon this point in a future lecture, and in its proper place.

I was endeavoring to establish the position that all language depends upon permanent principles; that words are the signs of ideas, and ideas are the impressions of things communicated to the mind thro the medium of some one of the five senses. I think I have succeeded so far as simple material things are concerned, to the satisfaction of all who have heard me. It may, perhaps, be more difficult for me to explain the words employed to express complex ideas, and things of immateriality, such as mind, and its attributes. But the rules previously adopted will, I apprehend, apply with equal ease and correctness in this case; and we shall have cause to admire the simple yet sublime foundation upon which the whole superstructure of language is based.

In pursuing this investigation I shall endeavor to avoid all abstruse and metaphysical reasoning, present no wild conjectures, or vain hypotheses; but confine myself to plain, common place matter of fact. We have reason to rejoice that a wonderful improvement in the science and cultivation of the mind has taken place in these last days; that we are no longer puzzled with the strange phantoms, the wild speculations which occupied the giant minds of a Descartes, a Malebranch, a Locke, a Reid, a Stewart, and hosts of others, whose shining talents would have qualified them for the brightest ornaments of literature, real benefactors of mankind, had not their education lead them into dark and metaphysical reasonings, a continued tissue of the wildest vagaries, in which they became entangled, till, at length, they were entirely lost in the labyrinth of their own conjectures.

The occasion of all their difficulty originated in an attempt to investigate the faculties of the mind without any means of getting at it. They did not content themselves with an adoption of the principles which lay at the foundation of all true philosophy, viz., that the facts to be accounted for, *do exist*; that truth is eternal, and we are to become acquainted with it by the means employed for its development. They quitted the world of materiality they inhabited, refused to examine the development of mind as the effect of an existing cause; and at one bold push, entered the world of thought, and made the unhallowed attempt to reason, a priori, concerning things which can only be known by their manifestations. But they soon found themselves in a strange land, confused with sights and sounds unknown, in the *explanation* of which they, of course, choose terms as unintelligible to their readers, as the *ideal realities* were to them. This course, adopted by Aristotle, has been too closely followed by those who have come after him. [2] But a new era has dawned upon the philosophy of the mind, and a corresponding change in the method of inculcating the principles of language must follow.[3]

In all our investigations we must take things as we find them, and account for them as far as we can. It would be a thankless task to attempt a change of principles in any thing. That would be an encroachment of the Creator's rights. It belongs to mortals to use the things they have as not abusing them;

and to Deity to regulate the laws by which those things are governed. And that man is the wisest, the truest philosopher, and brightest Christian, who acquaints himself with those laws as they do exist in the regulation of matter and mind, in the promotion of physical and moral enjoyment, and endeavors to conform to them in all his thoughts and actions.

From this apparent digression you will at once discover our object. We must not endeavor to change the principles of language, but to understand and explain them; to ascertain, as far as possible, the actions of the mind in obtaining ideas, and the use of language in expressing them. We may not be able to make our sentiments understood; but if they are not, the fault will originate in no obscurity in the facts themselves, but in our inability either to understand them or the words employed in their expression. Having been in the habit of using words with either no meaning or a wrong one, it may be difficult to comprehend the subject of which they treat. A man may have a quantity of sulphur, charcoal, and nitre, but it is not until he learns their properties and combinations that he can make gunpowder. Let us then adopt a careful and independent course of reasoning, resolved to meddle with nothing we do not understand, and to use no words until we know their meaning.

A complex idea is a combination of several simple ones, as a tree is made up of roots, a trunk, branches, twigs, and leaves. And these again may be divided into the wood, the bark, the sap, &c. Or we may employ the botanical terms, and enumerate its external and internal parts and qualities; the whole anatomy and physiology, as well as variety and history of trees of that species, and show its characteristic distinctions; for the mind receives a different impression on looking at a maple, a birch, a poplar, a tamarisk, a sycamore, or hemlock. In this way complex ideas are formed, distinct in their parts, but blended in a common whole; and, in conformity with the law regulating language, words, sounds or signs, are employed to express the complex whole, or each distinctive part. The same may be said of all things of like character. But this idea I will illustrate more at large before the close of this lecture.

First impressions are produced by a view of material things, as we have already seen; and the notion of action is obtained from a knowledge of the changes these things undergo. The idea of quality and definition is produced by contrast and comparison. Children soon learn the difference between a sweet apple and a sour one, a white rose and a red one, a hard seat and a soft one, harmonious sounds and those that are discordant, a pleasant smell and one that is disagreeable. As the mind advances, the application is varied, and they speak of a sweet rose, changing from *taste* and *sight* to smell, of a sweet song, of a hard apple, &c. According to the qualities thus learned, you may talk to them intelligibly of the *sweetness* of an apple, the *color* of a rose, the *hardness* of iron, the *harmony* of sounds, the *smell* or scent of things which possess that quality. As these agree or disagree with their comfort, they will call them *good* or *bad*, and speak of the qualities of goodness and badness, as if possessed by the thing itself.

In this apparently indiscriminate use of words, the ideas remain distinct; and each sign or object calls them up separately and associates them together, till, at length, in the single object is associated all the ideas entertained of its size, qualities, relations, and affinities.

In this manner, after long, persevering toil, principles of thought are fixed, and a foundation laid for the whole course of future thinking and speaking. The ideas become less simple and distinct. Just as fast as the mind advances in the knowledge of things, language keeps pace with the ideas, and even goes beyond them, so that in process of time a single term will not unfrequently represent a complexity of ideas, one of which will signify a whole combination of things.

On the other hand, there are many instances where the single declaration of a fact may convey to the untutored mind, a single thought or nearly so, when the better cultivated will take into the account the whole process by which it is effected. To illustrate: *a man killed a deer*. Here the boy would see and imagine more than he is yet fully able to comprehend. He will see the obvious fact that the man levels his musket, the gun goes off with a loud report, and the deer falls and dies. How this is all produced he does not understand, but knowing the fact he asserts the single truth—the man killed the deer. As the child advances, he will learn that the sentence conveys to the mind more than he at first perceived. He now understands how it was accomplished. The man had a gun. Then he must go back to the gunsmith and see how it was made, thence back to the iron taken from its bed, and wrought into bars; all the processes by which it is brought into the shape of a gun, the tools and machinery employed; the wood for the stock, its quality and production; the size, form and color of the lock, the principle upon which it moves; the flint, the effect produced by a collision with the steel, or a percussion cap, and its composition; till he finds a single gun in the hands of a man. The man is present with this gun. The motives which brought him here; the movements of his limbs, regulated by the determinations of the mind, and a thousand other such thoughts, might be taken into the account. Then the deer, his size, form, color, manner of living, next may claim a passing thought. But I need not enlarge. Here they both stand. The man has just seen the deer. As quick as thought his eye passes over the ground, sees the prey is within proper distance, takes aim, pulls the trigger, that loosens a spring, which forces the flint against the steel; this produces a spark, which ignites the charcoal, and the sulphur and nitre combined, explode and force the wad, which forces the ball from the gun, and is borne thro the air till it reaches the deer, enters his body by displacing the skin and flesh, deranges the animal functions, and death ensues. The whole and much more is expressed in the single phrase, "a man killed a deer."

It would be needless for me to stop here, and examine all the operations of the mind in coming at this state of knowledge. That is not the object of the present work. Such a duty belongs to another treatise, which may some day be undertaken, on logic and the science of the mind. The hint here given will enable you to perceive how the mind expands, and how language keeps pace with every advancing step, and, also, how combinations are made from simple things, as a house is made of timber, boards, shingles, nails, and paints; or of bricks, stone, and mortar; as the case may be, and when completed, a single term may express the idea, and you speak of a wood, or a brick house. Following this suggestion, by tracing the operations of the mind in the young child, or your own, very minutely, in the acquisition of any knowledge before wholly unknown to you, as a new language, or a new science; botany, mineralogy, chemistry, or phrenology; you will readily discover how the mind receives new impressions of things, and a new vocabulary is adopted to express the ideas formed of plants, minerals, chemical properties, and the development of the capacities of the mind as depending on material organs; how these things are changed and combined; and how their existence and qualities, changes and combinations, are expressed by words, to be retained, or conveyed to other minds.

But suppose you talk to a person wholly unacquainted with these things, will he understand you? Talk to him of stamens, pistils, calyxes; of monandria, diandria, triandria; of gypsum, talc, calcareous spar, quartz, topaz, mica, garnet, pyrites, hornblende, augite, actynolite; of hexahedral, prismatic, rhomboidal, dodecahedral; of acids and alkalies; of oxygen, hydrogen, nitrogen and carbon; of the configuration of the brain, and its relative powers; do all this, and what will he know of your meaning? So of all science. Words are to be understood from the things they are employed to represent. You may as well talk to a man in the hebrew, chinese, or choctaw languages, as in our own, if he does not know what is signified by the words selected as the medium of thought.

Your language may be most pure, perfect, full of meaning, but you cannot make yourself understood till your hearers can look thro your signs to the things signified. You may as well present before them a picture of *nothing*.

The great fault in the popular system of education is easily accounted for, particularly in reference to language. Children are taught to study signs without looking at the thing signified. In this way they are mere copyists, and the mind can never expand so as to make them independent, original thinkers. In fact, they can, in this way, never learn to reason well or employ language correctly; no more than a painter can be successful in his art, by merely looking at the pictures of others without having ever seen the originals. A good artist is a close observer of nature. So children should be left free to examine and reflect, and the signs will then serve their proper use—the means of acquiring the knowledge of things. In vain you may give a scholar a knowledge of the Hebrew, Greek, or Latin, learn him to translate with rapidity or speak our own language fluently. If he has not thereby learned the knowledge of things signified by such language, he is, in principle, advanced no farther than the parrot which says "pretty poll, pretty poll."

I am happy, however, in the consideration that a valuable change is taking place in this respect. Geography is no longer taught on the old systems, but maps are given to represent more vividly land and water, rivers, islands, and mountains. The study of arithmetic, chemistry, and nearly all the sciences have been materially improved within a few years. Grammar alone remains in quiet possession of its unquestioned authority. Its nine "parts of speech," its three genders, its three cases, its half dozen kinds of pronouns, and as many moods and tenses, have rarely been disquieted. A host of book makers have fondled around them, but few have dared molest them, finding them so snugly ensconced under the sanctity of age, and the venerated opinions of learned and good men. Of the numberless attempts to simplify grammar, what has been the success? Wherein do modern "simplifiers" differ from Murray? and he was only a *compiler*! They have all discovered his errors. But who has corrected them? They have all deviated somewhat from his manner. But what is that but saying, that with all his grammatical knowledge, he could not explain his own meaning?

All the trouble originates in this; the rules of grammar have not been sought for where they are only to be found, in the laws that govern matter and thought. Arbitrary rules have been adopted which will never apply in practice, except in special cases, and the attempt to bind language down to them is as absurd as to undertake to chain thought, or stop the waters of Niagara with a straw. Language will go on, and keep pace with the mind, and grammar should explain it so as to be correctly understood.

I wish you to keep these principles distinctly in view all thro my remarks, that you may challenge every position I assume till proved to be correct— till you distinctly understand it and definite impressions are made upon your minds. In this way you will discover a beauty and perfection in language before unknown; its rules will be found few and simple, holding with most unyielding tenacity to the sublime principles upon which they depend; and you will have reason to admire the works and adore the character of the great Parent Intellect, whose presence and protection pervade all his works and regulate the laws of matter and mind. You will feel yourselves involuntarily filled with sentiments of gratitude for the gift of mind, its affections, powers, and means of operation and communication, and resolved more than ever to employ these faculties in human improvement and the advancement of general happiness.

LECTURE III.

WRITTEN AND SPOKEN LANGUAGE.

Principles never alter. — They should be known. — Grammar a most important branch of science. — Spoken and written Language. — Idea of a thing. — How expressed. — An example. — Picture writing. — An anecdote. — Ideas expressed by actions. — Principles of spoken and written Language. — Apply universally. — Two examples. — English language. — Foreign words. — Words in science. — New words. — How formed.

We now come to take a nearer view of language as generally understood by grammar. But we shall have no occasion to depart from the principles already advanced, for there is existing in practice nothing which may not be accounted for in theory; as there can be no effect without an efficient cause to produce it.

We may, however, long remain ignorant of the true explanation of the principles involved; but the fault is ours, and not in the things themselves. The earth moved with as much grandeur and precision around its axis and in its orbit before the days of Gallileo Gallilei, when philosophers believed it flat and stationary, as it has done since. So the great principles on which depends the existence and use of all language are permanent, and may be correctly employed by those who have never examined them; but this does not prove that to be ignorant is better than to be wise. We may have taken food all our days without knowing much of the process by which it is converted into nourishment and incorporated into our bodies, without ever having heard of delutition chymification, chylification, or even digestion, as a whole; but this is far from convincing me that the knowledge of these things is unimportant, or that ignorance of them is not the cause of much disease and suffering among mankind. And it is, or should be, the business of the physiologist to explain these things, and show the great practical benefit resulting from a general knowledge of them. So the grammarian should act as a sort of physiologist of language. He should analyze all its parts and show how it is framed together to constitute a perfect whole.

Instead of exacting of you a blind submission to a set of technical expressions, and arbitrary rules, I most urgently exhort you to continue, with unremitting assiduity, your inquiries into the reason and propriety of the positions which may be taken. It is the business of philosophy, not to meddle with things to direct how they should be, but to account for them and their properties and relations as they are. So it is the business of grammar to explain language as it exists in use, and exhibit the reason why it is used thus, and what principles must be observed to employ it correctly in speaking and writing. This method is adopted to carry out the principles already established, and show their adaptation to the wants of the community, and how they may be correctly and successfully employed. Grammar considered in this light forms a department in the science of the mind by no means unimportant. And it can not fail to be deeply interesting to all who would employ it in the business, social, literary, moral, or religious concerns of life. Those who have thoughts to communicate, or desire an acquaintance with the minds of others, can not be indifferent to the means on which such intercourse depends. I am convinced, therefore, that you will give me your most profound attention as I pursue the subject of the present lecture somewhat in detail. And I hope you will not consider me tedious or unnecessarily prolix in my remarks.

I will not be particular in my remarks upon the changes of spoken and written language, altho that topic of itself, in the different sounds and signs employed in different ages and by different nations to express the same idea, would form a most interesting theme for several lectures. But that work must be reserved for a future occasion. You are all acquainted with the signs, written and spoken, which are employed in our language as vehicles (some of them like omnibusses) of thought to carry ideas from one mind to another. Some of you doubtless are acquainted with the application of this fact in other languages. In other words, you know how to sound the name of a thing, how to describe its properties as far as you understand them, and its attitudes or changes. This you can do by vocal sounds, or written, or printed signs.

On the other hand, you can receive a similar impression by hearing the description of another, or by seeing it written or printed. But here you will bear in mind the fact that the word, spoken or written, is but the sign of the idea derived from the thing signified. For example: Here is an apple. I do not now speak of its composition, the skin, the pulp, &c.; nor of its qualities, whether sour, or sweet, or bitter, good or bad, great or small, long or short, round or flat, red, or white, or yellow. I speak of a single thing—an apple. Here it is, present before you. Look at it. It is now removed. You do not see it. Your minds are occupied with something else, in looking at that organ, or this representation of Solomon's temple, or, perhaps, lingering in melancholy review of your old systems of grammar thro which you plodded at a tedious rate, goaded on by the stimulus of the ferule, or the fear of being called ignorant. From that unhappy reverie I recal your minds, by saying *apple*. An apple? where? There is none in sight. No; but you have distinct recollections of a single object I just now held before you. You see it, mentally, and were you painters you might paint its likeness. What has brought this object so vividly before you? The single sound *apple*. This sound has called up the idea produced in your mind on looking at this object which I now again present before you. Here is the thing represented —the apple. Again I lay it aside, and commence a conversation with you on the varieties of apples, the form, color, flavor, manner of production, their difference from other fruit, where found, when, and by whom. Here! look again. What do you see? A-P-P-L-E—*Apple*. What is that? The representation of the idea produced in the mind by a certain object you saw a little while ago. Here then you have the spoken and written signs of this single object I now again present to your vision. This idea may also be called up by the sense of feeling, smelling, or tasting, under certain restrictions. Here you would be no more liable to be mistaken than by seeing. We can indeed imagine things which would feel, and smell, and taste, and look some like an apple, but it falls to the lot of more abstruse reasoners to make their suppositions, and then account for them—to imagine things, and then treat of them as realities. We are content with the knowledge of things as they do exist, and think there is little danger of mistaking a potato for an apple, or a squash for a pear. Tho in the dark we may lay hold of the Frenchman's *pomme de terre*—apple of the earth, the first bite will satisfy us of our mistake if we are not too metaphysical.

The same idea may be called up in your minds by a picture of the apple presented to your sight. On this ground the picture writing of the ancients may be accounted for; and after that, the hieroglyphics of Egypt and other countries, which was but a step from picture writing towards the use of the alphabet. But these signs or vehicles for the conveyance or transmission of their thoughts, compared with the present perfect state of language, were as aukward and uncomly as the carriages employed for the conveyance of their bodies were compared with those now in use. They were like ox carts drawn by mules, compared with the most splendid barouches drawn by elegant dapple-greys.

A similar mode would be adopted now by those unacquainted with alphabetical writing. It was so with the merchant who could not write. He sold his neighbor a grindstone, on trust. Lest he should forget it—lest the *idea* of it should be obliterated from the mind—he, in the absence of his clerk, took his book and a pen and drew out a *round picture* to represent it. Some months after, he dunned his neighbor for his pay for a cheese. "I have bought no cheese of you," was the reply. Yes, you have, for I have it charged. "You must be mistaken, for I never bought a cheese. We always make our own." How then should I have one charged to you? "I cannot tell. I have never had any thing here on credit except a grindstone." Ah! that's it, that's it, only I forgot to make a hole through it!"

Ideas may also be exchanged by actions. This is the first and strongest language of nature. It may be employed, when words have failed, in the most effectual manner. The angry man, choked with rage, unable to speak, tells the violent passions, burning in his bosom, in a language which can not be mistaken. The actions of a friend are a surer test of friendship than all the honied words he may utter. Actions speak louder than words. The first impressions of maternal affection are produced in the infant mind by the soothing attentions of the mother. In the same way we may understand the language of the deaf and dumb. Certain motions express certain ideas. These being duly arranged and conformed to our alphabetic signs, and well understood, the pupil may become acquainted with book knowledge as well as we. They go by sight and not by sound. A different method is adopted with the blind. Letters with them are so arranged that they can *feel* them. The signs thus felt correspond with the sounds they hear. Here they must stop. They cannot see to describe. Those who are so unfortunate as to be blind and deaf, can have but a faint knowledge of language, or the ideas of others.

On similar principles we may explain the pantomime plays sometimes performed, where the most entertaining scenes of love and murder are represented, but not a word spoken.

Three things are always to be born in mind in the use and study of all language: 1st, the thing signified; 2d, the idea of the thing; and 3d, the word or sign chosen to represent it.

Things exist.

Thinking beings conceive *ideas of things.*

Those who employ language adopt *sounds or signs to convey those ideas* to others.

On these obvious principles rest the whole superstructure of all language, spoken or written. Objects are presented to the mind, impressions are there made, which, retained, constitute the idea, and, by agreement, certain words are employed as the future signs or representations of those ideas. If we saw an object in early life and knew its *name*, the mention of that name will recal afresh the idea which had long lain dormant in the memory, (if I may so speak,) and we can converse about it as correctly as when we first saw it.

These principles, I have said, hold good in all languages. Proof of this may not improperly be offered here, provided it be not too prolix. I will endeavor to be brief.

In an open area of sufficient dimensions is congregated a delegation from every language under heaven. All are so arranged as to face a common center. A white horse is led into that spot and all look at the living animal which stands before them. The same impression must be made on all minds so far as a single animal is concerned. But as the whole is made up of parts, so their minds will soon diverge from a single idea, and one will think of his size, compared with other horses; another of his form; another of his color. Some will think of his noble appearance, others of his ability to travel, or (in jockey phrase) his *speed*. The farrier will look for his blemishes, to see if he is *sound*, and the jockey at his teeth, to *guess* at his *age*. The anatomist will, in thought, dissect him into parts and see every bone, sinew, cartilage, blood vessel, his stomach, lungs, liver, heart, entrails; every part will be laid open; and while the thoughtless urchin sees a single object—a white horse —others will, at a single glance, read volumes of instruction. Oh! the importance of knowledge! how little is it regarded! What funds of instruction might be gathered from the lessons every where presented to the mind!

One impression would be made on all minds in reference to the single tangible object before them; no matter how learned or ignorant. There stands an animal obvious to all. Let him be removed out of sight, and a very exact picture of him suspended in his place. All again agree. Here then is the proof of our first general principle, viz. all language depends on the fixed and unvarying laws of nature.

Let the picture be removed and a man step forth and pronounce the word, *ippos*. The Greek starts up and says, "Yes, it is so." The rest do not comprehend him. He then writes out distinctly, ΙΠΠΟΣ. They are in the dark as to the meaning. They know not whether a horse, a man, or a goose is named. All the Greeks, however, understand the meaning the same as when the horse or picture was before them, for they had *agreed* that *ippos* should represent the *idea* of that animal.

Forth steps another, and pronounces the word *cheval*. Every Frenchman is aroused: Oui, monsieur? Yes, sir. Comprenez vous? Do you understand? he says to the rest. But they are dumb. He then writes C-H-E-V-A-L. All are as ignorant as before, save the Frenchmen who had agreed that *cheval* should be the name for horse.

Next go yourself, thinking all will understand you, and say, *horse*; but, lo! none unacquainted with your language are the wiser for the sound you utter, or the sign you suspended before them; save, perhaps, a little old Saxon, who, at first looks deceived by the similarity of sound, but, seeing the sign, is as demure as ever, for he omits the *e*, and pronounces it shorter than we do, more like a yorkshire man. But why are you not understood? Because others have not entered into an *agreement* with you that *h-o-r-s-e*, spoken or written, shall represent that animal.

Take another example. Place the living animal called man before them. Less trouble will be found in this case than in the former, for there is a nearer agreement than before in regard to the signs which shall be employed to express the idea. This word occurs with very little variation in the modern languages, derived undoubtedly from the Teutonic, with a little change in the spelling, as Saxon *mann* or *mon*, Gothic *manna*, German, Danish, Dutch, Swedish and Icelandic like ours. In the south of Europe, however, this word varies as well as others.

Our language is derived more directly from the old Saxon than from any other, but has a great similarity to the French and Latin, and a kind of cousin-german to all the languages of Europe, ancient and modern. Ours, indeed, is a compound from most other languages, retaining some of their beauties and many of their defects. We can boast little distinctive character of our own. As England was possessed by different nations at different periods, so different dialects were introduced, and we can trace our language to as many sources, German, Danish, Saxon, French, and Roman, which were the different nations amalgamated into the British empire. We retain little of the real old english—few words which may not be traced to a foreign extraction. Different people settling in a country would of course carry their ideas and manner of expressing them; and from the whole compound a general agreement would, in process of time, take place, and a uniform language be established. Such is the origin and condition of our language, as well as every other modern tongue of which we have any knowledge.

There is one practice of which our savans are guilty, at which I do most seriously demur—the extravagant introduction of exotic words into our vocabulary, apparently for no other object than to swell the size of a dictionary, and boast of having found out and defined thousands of words more than any body else. A mania seems to have seized our lexicographers, so that they have forsaken the good old style of "plainness of speech," and are flourishing and brandishing about in a cloud of verbiage as though the whole end of instruction was to teach loquacity. And some of our popular writers and speakers have caught the infection, and flourish in borrowed garments, prizing themselves most highly when they use words and phrases which no body can understand.

I will not contend that in the advancement of the arts and sciences it may not be proper to introduce foreign terms as the mean of conveying a knowledge of those improvements to others. It is better than to coin new words, inasmuch as they are generally adopted by all modern nations. In this way all languages are approximating together; and when the light of truth, science, and religion, has fully shone on all the nations, we may hope one language will be spoken, and the promise be fulfilled, that God has "turned unto the people a pure language, that they may call upon the name of the Lord, to serve him with one consent."

New ideas are formed like new inventions. Established principles are employed in a new combination, so as to produce a new manifestation. Words are chosen as nearly allied to former ideas as possible, to express or represent this new combination. Thus, Fulton applied steam power to navigation. A new idea was produced. A boat was seen passing along the waters without the aid of wind or tide. Instead of coining a new word to express the whole, a word which nobody would understand, two old ones were combined, and "*steamboat*" became the sign to represent the idea of the thing beheld. So with rail-road, cotton-mill, and gun-powder. In the same way we may account for most words employed in science, although in that case we are more dependant on foreign languages, in as much as a large portion of our knowledge is derived from them. But we may account for them on the same principle as above. *Phrenology* is a compound of two greek words, and means the science or knowledge of the mind. So of geology, mineralogy, &c. But when improvements are made by those who speak the english, words in our own language are employed and used not only by ourselves, but also by those nations who profit by our investigations.

I trust I have now said enough on the general principles of language as applied to things. In the next lecture I will come down to a sort of bird's eye view of grammar. But my soul abhors arbitrary rules so devoutly, I can make no promises how long I will continue in close communion with set forms of speech. I love to wander too well to remain confined to one spot, narrowed up in the limits fixed by others. Freedom is the empire of the mind; it abjures all fetters, all slavery. It kneels at the altar of virtue and worships at the shrine of truth. No obstacles should be thrown in the way of its progress. No limits should be set to it but those of the Almighty.

LECTURE IV.

ON NOUNS.

Nouns defined. — Things. — Qualities of matter. — Mind. — Spiritual beings. — Qualities of mind. — How learned. — Imaginary things. — Negation. — Names of actions. — Proper nouns. — Characteristic names. — Proper nouns may become common.

Your attention is, this evening, invited to the first divisions of words, called *Nouns*. This is a most important class, and as such deserves our particular notice.

Nouns are the names of things.

The word *noun* is derived from the Latin *nomen*, French *nom*. It means *name*. Hence the definition above given.

In grammar it is employed to distinguish that class of words which name things, or stand as signs or representatives of things.

We use the word *thing* in its broadest sense, including every possible entity; every being, or thing, animate or inanimate, material or immaterial, real or imaginary, physical, moral, or intellectual. It is the noun of the Saxon *thincan* or *thingian*, to think; and is used to express every conceivable object of thought, in whatever form or manner presented to the human mind.

Every word employed to designate things, or name them, is to be ranked in the class called *nouns*, or names. You have only to determine whether a word is used thus, to learn whether it belongs to this or some other class of words. Here let me repeat:

1. Things exist.
2. We conceive ideas of things.

3. We use sounds or signs to communicate these ideas to others.
4. We denominate the class of words thus used, *nouns*.

Perhaps I ought to stop here, or pass to another topic. But as these lectures are intended to be so plain that all can understand my meaning, I must indulge in a few more remarks before advancing farther.

In addition to individual, tangible objects, we conceive ideas of the *qualities* of things, and give *names* to such qualities, which become *nouns*. Thus, the *hardness* of iron, the *heat* of fire, the *color* of a rose, the *bitterness* of gall, the *error* of grammars. The following may serve to make my views more plain. Take two tumblers, the one half filled with water, the other with milk; mix them together. You can now talk of the milk in the water, or the water in the milk. Your ideas are distinct, tho the objects are so intimately blended, that they can not be separated. So with the qualities of things.

We also speak of mind, intellect, soul; but to them we can give no form, and of them paint no likeness. Yet we have ideas of them, and employ words to express them, which become *nouns*.

This accounts for the reason why the great Parent Intellect has strictly forbidden, in the decalogue, that a likeness of him should be constructed. His being and attributes are discoverable only thro the medium of his works and word. No man can see him and live. It would be the height of folly—it would be more—it would be blasphemy—to attempt to paint the likeness of him whose presence fills immensity—whose center is every where, and whose circumference is no where. The name of this Spirit or Being was held in the most profound reverence by the Jews, as we shall have occasion to mention when we come to treat of the verb TO BE.

We talk of angels, and have seen the unhallowed attempt to describe their likeness in the form of pictures, which display the fancy of the artist very finely, but give a miserable idea of those pure spirits who minister at the altar of God, and chant his praises in notes of the most unspeakable delight.

We have also seen *death* and the pale horse, the firy dragon, the mystery of Babylon, and such like things, represented on canvass; but they betoken more of human talent to depict the marvellous, than a strict regard for truth. Beelzebub, imps, and all Pandemonium, may be vividly imagined and finely arranged in fiction, and we can name them. Wizzards, witches, and fairies, may play their sportive tricks in the human brain, and receive names as tho they were real.

We also think and speak of the qualities and affections of the mind as well as matter, as wisdom, knowledge, virtue, vice, love, hatred, anger. Our conceptions in this case may be less distinct, but we have ideas, and use words to express them. There is, we confess, a greater liability to mistake and misunderstand when treating of mind and its qualities, than of matter. The reason is evident, people know less of it. Its operations are less distinct and more varying.

The child first sees material objects. It is taught to name them. It next learns the qualities of things; as the sweetness of sugar, the darkness of night, the beauty of flowers. From this it ascends by gradation to the higher attainments of knowledge as revealed in the empire of mind, as well as matter. Great care should be taken that this advancement be easy, natural, and thoro. It should be constantly impressed with the importance of obtaining clear and definite ideas of things, and never employ words till it has ideas to express; never name a thing of which it has no knowledge. This is ignorance.

It would be well, perhaps, to extend this remark to those older than children, in years, but less in real practical knowledge. The remark is of such general application, that no specification need be made, except to the case before us; to those affected proficients in grammar, whose only knowledge is the memory of words, which to them have no meanings, if, indeed, the writers themselves had any to express by them; a fact we regard as questionable, at best. There is hardly a teacher of grammar, whose self-esteem is not enormous, who will not confess himself ignorant on many of the important principles of language; that he has never understood, and could never explain them. He finds no difficulty in repeating what the books say, but if called upon to express an opinion of his own, he has none to give. He has learned and used words without knowing their meaning.

Children should be taught language as they are taught music. They should learn the simple tones on which the whole science depends. Distinct impressions of sounds should be made on their minds, and the characters which represent them should be inseparably associated with them. They will then learn tunes from the compositions of those sounds, as represented by notes. By dint of application, they will soon become familiar with these principles, if possessed of a talent for song, and may soon pass the acme with ease, accuracy, and rapidity. But there are those who may sing very prettily, and tolerably correct, who have never studied the first rudiments of music. But such can never become adepts in the science.

So there are those who use language correctly, who never saw the inside of a grammar book, and who never examined the principles on which it depends. But this, by no means, proves that it is better to sing by rote, than "with the understanding." These rudiments, however, should form the business of the nursery, rather than the grammar school. Every mother should labor to give distinct and forcible impressions of such things as she learns her children to *name*. She should carefully prevent them from employing words which have no meaning, and still more strictly should she guard them against attaching a wrong meaning to those they do use. In this way, the foundation for future knowledge and eminence, would be laid broad and deep. But I wander.

We attach names to imaginary things; as ghosts, genii, imps.

To this class belong the thirty thousand gods of the ancients, who were frequently represented by emblems significant of the characters attached to them. We employ words to name these imaginary things, so that we read and converse about them understandingly, tho our ideas may be exceedingly various.

Nouns are also used to express negation, of which no idea can be formed. In this case, the mind rests on what exists, and employs a word to express what does not. We speak of *a hole* in the paper. But we can form no idea of *a hole*, separated from the surrounding substances. Remove the parts of the paper till nothing is left, and then you may look in vain for the hole. It is not there. It never was. In the same way we use the words nothing, nobody, nonentity, vacuum, absence, space, blank, annihilation, and oblivion. These are relative terms, to be understood in reference to things which are known to exist. We must know of *some*thing before we can talk of *no*thing, of an entity before we can think of nonentity.

In a similar way we employ words to name actions, which are produced by the changes of objects. We speak of a race, of a flight, of a sitting or session, of a journey, of a ride, of a walk, of a residence, etc. In all these cases, the mind is fixed on the persons who performed these things. Take for example, a race. Of that, we can conceive no idea separate from the agent or object which *ran* the *race*. Without some other word to inform us we could not decide whether a *horse* race, a *foot* race, a boat race, the race of a mill, or some other race, was the object of remark. The same may be said of flight, for we read of the flight of birds, the flight of Mahommed, the flight of armies, and the flight of intellect.

We also give names to actions as tho they were taking place in the present tense. "The *reading* of the report was deferred;" steamboat *racing* is dangerous to public safety; *stealing* is a crime; false *teaching* deserves the reprobation of all.

The hints I have given will assist you in acquiring a knowledge of nouns as used to express ideas in vocal or written language. This subject might be pursued further with profit, if time would permit. As the time allotted to this lecture is nearly exhausted, I forbear. I shall hereafter have occasion to show how a whole phrase may be used to name an idea, and as such stand as the agent or object of a verb.

Some nouns are specifically used to designate certain objects, and distinguish them from the class to which they usually belong. In this way they assume a distinctive character, and are usually denominated PROPER NOUNS. They apply to persons, places and things; as, John Smith, Boston, Hylax. *Boy* is applied in common to all young males of the human species, and as such is a *common noun* or name. *John Smith* designates a particular boy from the rest.

Proper names may be also applied to animals and things. The stable keeper and stageman has a name for every horse he owns, to distinguish it from other horses; the dairyman for his cows, the boy for his dog, and the girl for her doll. Any word, in fact, may become a proper name by being specifically used; as the ship Fair Trader, the brig Success, sloop Delight in Peace, the race horse Eclipse, Black Hawk, Round Nose, and Red Jacket.

Proper names were formerly used in reference to certain traits of character or circumstances connected with the place or thing. *Abram* was changed to *Abraham*, the former signifying *an elevated father*, the latter, *the father of a multitude*. *Isaac* signified *laughter*, and was given because his mother laughed at the message of the angel. *Jacob* signified *a supplanter*, because he was to obtain the birthright of his elder brother.

A ridiculous rage obtained with our puritan fathers to express scripture sentiments in the names of their children, as may be seen by consulting the records of the Plymouth and Massachusetts colonies.

This practice has not wholly gone out of use in our day, for we hear of the names of Hope, Mercy, Patience, Comfort, Experience, Temperance, Faith, Deliverance, Return, and such like, applied usually to females, (being more in character probably,) and sometimes to males. We have also the names of White, Black, Green, Red, Gray, Brown, Olive, Whitefield, Blackwood, Redfield, Woodhouse, Stonehouse, Waterhouse, Woodbridge, Swiftwater, Lowater, Drinkwater, Spring, Brooks, Rivers, Pond, Lake, Fairweather, Merryweather, Weatherhead, Rice, Wheat, Straw, Greatrakes, Bird, Fowle, Crow, Hawks, Eagle, Partridge, Wren, Goslings, Fox, Camel, Zebra, Bear, Wolf, Hogg, Rain, Snow, Haile, Frost, Fogg, Mudd, Clay, Sands, Hills, Valley, Field, Stone, Flint, Silver, Gould, and Diamond.

Proper nouns may also become common when used as words of general import; as, *dunces*, corrupted from Duns Scotus, a distinguished theologian, born at Dunstane, Northumberland, an opposer of the doctrines of Thomas Aquinus. He is a real *solomon*, jack tars, judases, antichrist, and so on.

Nouns may also be considered in respect to person, number, gender, and positive, or case. There are *three* persons, *two* numbers, *two* genders, and *two* cases. But the further consideration of these things will be deferred, which, together with Pronouns, will form the subject of our next lecture.

LECTURE V.

ON NOUNS AND PRONOUNS.

Nouns in respect to persons. — Number. — Singular. — Plural. — How formed. — Foreign plurals. — Proper names admit of plurals. — Gender. — No neuter. — In figurative language. — Errors. — Position or case. — Agents. — Objects. — Possessive case considered. — A definitive word. — Pronouns. — One kind. — Originally nouns. — Specifically applied.

We resume the consideration of nouns this evening, in relation to person, number, gender, and position or case.

In the use of language there is a speaker, person spoken to, and things spoken of. Those who speak are the *first* persons, those who hear the *second*, and those who are the subject of conversation the *third*.

The first and second persons are generally used in reference to human beings capable of speech and understanding. But we sometimes condesend to hold converse with animals and inanimate matter. The bird trainer talks to his parrots, the coachman to his horses, the sailor to the winds, and the poet to his landscapes, towers, and wild imaginings, to which he gives a "local habitation and a name."

By metaphor, language is put into the mouths of animals, particularly in fables. By a still further license, places and things, flowers, trees, forests, brooks, lakes, mountains, towers, castles, stars, &c. are made to speak the most eloquent language, in the first person, in addresses the most pathetic. The propriety of such a use of words I will not stop to question, but simply remark that such figures should never be employed in the instruction of children. As the mind expands, no longer content to grovel amidst mundane things, we mount the pegasus of imagination and soar thro the blissful or terrific scenes of fancy and fiction, and study a language before unknown.

But it would be an unrighteous demand upon others, to require them to understand us; and quite as unpardonable to brand them with ignorance because they do not.

Most nouns are in the third person. More things are talked about than talk themselves, or are talked to by others. Hence there is little necessity for teaching children to specify except in the first or second person, which is very easily done.

In English there are two *numbers*, singular and plural. The singular is confined to one, the plural is extended to any indefinite number. The Greeks, adopted a dual number which they used to express two objects united in pairs, or couples; as, a span of horses, a yoke of oxen, a brace of pistols, a pair of shoes. We express the same idea with more words, using the singular to represent the union of the two. We also extend this use of words and employ what are called *nouns of multitude*; as, a people, an army, a host, a nation. These and similar words are used in the singular referring to many combined in a united whole, or in the plural comprehending a diversity; as, "the armies met," "the nations are at peace." *People* admits no change on account of number. We say "*many* people are collected together and form *a* numerous people."

The plural is not always to be understood as expressing an increase of number, but of qualities or sorts of things, as the merchant has a variety of *sugars, wines, teas, drugs, medicines, paints* and *dye-woods*. We also speak of *hopes, fears, loves, anxieties*.

Some nouns admit of no plural, in fact, or in use; as, chaos, universe, fitness, immortality, immensity, eternity. Others admit of no singular; as, scissors, tongs, vitals, molasses. These words probably once had singulars, but having no use for them they became obsolete. We have long been accustomed to associate the two halves of shears together, so that in speaking of one whole, we say shears, and of apart, half of a shears. But of some words originally, and in fact plural, we have formed a singular; as, "one twin died, and, tho the other one survived its dangerous illness, the mother wept bitterly for her twins." *Twin* is composed of *two* and *one*. It is found in old books, spelled *twane*, two-one, or twin. Thus, the *twi*-light is formed by the mingling of two lights, or the division of the rays of light by the approaching or receding darkness. They *twain* shall be one flesh. Sheep and deer are singular or plural.

Most plurals are formed by adding *s* to the singular, or, when euphony requires it, *es*; as, tree, trees; sun, suns; dish, dishes; box, boxes. Some retain the old plural form; as, ox, oxen; child, children; chick, chicken; kit, kitten. But habit has burst the barrier of old rules, and we now talk of chicks and chickens, kits and kittens. *Oxen* alone stands as a monument raised to the memory of unaltered saxon plurals.

Some nouns form irregular plurals. Those ending in *f* change that letter to *v* and then add *es*; as, half, halves; leaf, leaves; wolf, wolves. Those ending in *y* change that to *i* and add the *es*; as, cherry, cherries; berry, berries; except when the *y* is preceded by a vowel, in which case it only adds the *s*; as, day, days; money, moneys (not *ies*); attorney, attorneys. All this is to make the sound more easy and harmonious. *F* and *v* were formerly used indiscriminately, in singulars as well as plurals, and, in fact, in the composition of all words where they occurred. The same may be said of *i* and *y*.

> "The Fader (Father) Almychty of the heven abuf (above)
> In the mene tyme, unto Juno his *luf* (love)
> Thus spak; and sayd."
>
> *Douglas, booke 12, pag. 441.*

> "They lyued in ioye and in felycite
> For eche of hem had other lefe and dere."
>
> *Chaucer, Monks Tale, fol. 81, p. 1.*

> "When straite twane beefes he tooke
> And an the aultar layde."

The reason why *y* is changed into *i* in the formation of plurals, and in certain other cases, is, I apprehend, accounted for from the fact that words which now end in *y* formerly ended in *ie*, as may be seen in all old books. The regular plural was then formed by adding *s*.

"And upon those members of the *bodie*, which *wee* thinke most unhonest, put *wee* more honestie on." "It rejoyceth not in iniquitie—diversitie of gifts —all thinges edifie not." See old bible, 1 Cor., chap. 13 and 14.

Other words form their plurals still more differently, for which no other rule than habit can be given; as, man, men; foot, feet; tooth, teeth; die, dice; mouse, mice; penny, pence, and sometimes pennies, when applied to distinct pieces of money, and not to value.

Many foreign nouns retain the plural form as used by the nations from whom we have borrowed them; as, cherub, cherubim; seraph, seraphim; radius, radii; memorandum, memoranda; datum, data, &c. We should be pleased to have such words carried home, or, if they are ours by virtue of possession, let them be adopted into our family, and put on the garments of naturalized citizens, and no longer appear as lonely strangers among us. There is great aukwardness in adding the english to the hebrew plural of cherub, as the translators of the common version of the bible have done. They use *cherub* in the singular and cherub*ims* in the plural. The *s* should be omitted and the Hebrew plural retained, or the preferable course adopted, and the final *s* be added, making cherubs, seraphs, &c. The same might be said of all foreign nouns. It would add much to the regularity, dignity, and beauty, of our vernacular tongue.

Proper nouns admit of the plural number; as, there are sixty-four John Smiths in New-York, twenty Arnolds in Providence, and fifteen Davises in Boston. As we are not accustomed to form the plurals of proper names there is not that ease and harmony in the first use of them that we have found in those with which we are more familiar; especially those we have rarely heard pronounced. Habit surmounts the greatest obstacles and makes things the most harsh and unpleasant appear soft and agreeable.

Gender is applied to the distinction of the sexes. There are two—masculine and feminine. The former is applied to males, the latter to females. Those words which belong to neither gender, have been called *neuter*, that is, *no gender*. But it is hardly necessary to perplex the minds of learners with *negatives*. Let them distinguish between masculine and feminine genders, and little need be said to them about a *neuter*.

There are some nouns of both genders, as student, writer, pupil, person, citizen, resident. *Poet, author,* editor, and some other words, have of late been applied to females, instead of poet*ess,* author*ess,* edit*ress.* Fashion will soon preclude the necessity of this former distinction.

Some languages determine their genders by the form of the endings of their nouns, and what is thus made masculine in Rome, may be feminine in France. It is owing, no doubt, to this practice, in other nations, that we have attached the idea of gender to inanimate things; as, "the sun, *he* shines majestically;" while of the moon, it is said, "*she* sheds a milder radiance." But we can not coincide with the reason assigned by Mr. Murray, for this distinction. His notion is not valid. It does not correspond with facts. While in the south of Europe the sun is called masculine and the moon feminine, the northern nations invariably reverse the distinction, particularly the dialects of the Scandinavian. It was so in our own language in the time of Shakspeare. He calls the sun a "*fair wench.*"

By figures of rhetoric, genders may be attached to inanimate matter. Where things are personified, we usually speak of them as masculine and feminine; but this practice depends on fancy, and not on any fixed rules. There is, in truth, but two genders, and those confined to animals. When we break these rules, and follow the undirected wanderings of fancy, we can form no rules to regulate our words. We may have as many fanciful ones as we please, but they will not apply in common practice. For example: poets and artists have usually attached female loveliness to angels, and placed them in the feminine gender. But they are invariably used in the masculine thro out the scriptures.

There is an apparent absurdity in saying of the ship General Williams, *she* is beautiful; or, of the steamboat Benjamin Franklin, *she* is out of date. It were far better to use no gender in such cases. But if people will continue the practice of making distinctions where there are none, they must do it from habit and whim, and not from any reason or propriety.

There are three ways in which we usually distinguish the forms of words in reference to gender. 1st. By words which are different; as boy, girl; uncle, aunt; father, mother. 2d. By a different termination of the same word; as instructor, instructress; lion, lioness; poet, poetess. *Ess* is a contraction from the hebrew *essa*, a female. 3d. By prefixing another word; as, a male child, a female child; a man servant, a maid servant; a he-goat, a she-goat.

The last consideration that attaches to nouns, is the *position* they occupy in written or spoken language, in relation to other words, as being *agents*, or *objects* of action. This is termed *position*.

There are two positions in which nouns stand in reference to their meaning and use. First, as *agents* of action, as *David* killed Goliath. Second, as *objects* on which action terminates; as, *Richard* conquered *Henry*. These two distinctions should be observed in the use of all nouns. But the propriety of this division will be more evident when we come to treat of verbs, their agents and objects.

It will be perceived that we have abandoned the use of the "*possessive case*," a distinction which has been insisted on in our grammars; and also changed the names of the other two. As we would adopt nothing that is new without first being convinced that something is needed which the thing proposed will supply; so we would reject nothing that is old, till we have found it useless and cumbersome. It will be admitted on all hands that the fewer and simpler the rules of grammar, the more readily will they be understood, and the more correctly applied. We should guard, on the one hand, against having so many as to perplex, and on the other, retain enough to apply in the correct use of language. It is on this ground that we have proposed an improvement in the names and number of cases, or positions.

The word noun signifies name, and *nominative* is the adjective derived from noun, and partakes of the same meaning. Hence the *nominative* or *naming* case may apply as correctly to the object as the agent. "*John* strikes *Thomas*, and *Thomas* strikes *John*." John and Thomas name the boys who strike, but in the first case John is the actor or agent and Thomas the object. In the latter it is changed. To use a *nominative name* is a redundancy which should be avoided. You will understand my meaning and see the propriety of the change proposed, as the mind of the learner should not be burthened with needless or irrelevant phrases.

But our main objection lies against the "possessive case." We regard it as a false and unnecessary distinction. What is the possessive case? Murray defines it as "expressing the relation of property or possession; as, my father's house." His rule of syntax is, "one substantive governs another, signifying a different thing, in the possessive or genitive case; as, my father's house." I desire you to understand the definition and use as here given. Read it over again, and be careful that you know the meaning of *property*, *possession*, and *government*. Now let a scholar parse correctly the example given. "*Father's*" is a common noun, third person, singular number, masculine gender, and *governed* by house:" Rule, "One noun *governs* another," &c. Then my father does not govern his own house, but his house him! What must be the conduct and condition of the family, if they have usurped the government of their head? "John Jones, hatter, keeps constantly for sale all kinds of *boy's hats*. Parse boy's. It is a noun, possessive case, *governed* by hats." What is the possessive case? It "signifies the *relation of property or possession*." Do the hats belong to the boys? Oh no. Are they the *property* or in the *possession* of the boys? Certainly not. Then what relation is there of property or possession? None at all. They belong to John Jones, were made by him, are his property, and by him are advertised for sale. He has used the word *boy's* to distinguish their size, quality, and fitness for boy's use.

"The master's slave." Master's is in the possessive case, and *governed* by slave! If grammars are true there can be no need of abolition societies, unless it is to look after the master and see that he is not abused. The rider's horse; the captain's ship; the general's army; the governor's cat; the king's subject. How false it would be to teach scholars the idea of *property* and *government* in such cases. The *teacher's scholars* should never learn that by virtue of their grammars, or the *apostrophe* and letter *s*, they have a right to *govern* their teachers; nor the mother's son, to govern his mother. Our merchants would dislike exceedingly to have the *ladies* understand them to signify by their advertisements that the "ladies' merino shawls, the ladies's bonnets and lace wrought veils, the ladies' gloves and elegant Thibet, silk and challa dresses, were the *property* of the ladies; for in that case they might claim or *possess* themselves of their *property*, and no longer trouble the merchant with the care of it.

"Peter's wife's mother lay sick of a fever." "*His* physician said that *his* disease would require *his* utmost skill to defeat *its* progress in *his* limbs." Phrases like these are constantly occurring, which can not be explained intelligibly by the existing grammars. In fact, the words said to be nouns in the possessive case, have changed their character, by use, from nouns to adjectives, or definitive words, and should thus be classed. Russia iron, Holland gin, China ware, American people, the Washington tavern, Lafayette house, Astor house, Hudson river, (formerly Hudson's,) Baffin's bay, Van Dieman's land, John street, Harper's ferry, Hill's bridge, a paper book, a bound book, a red book, John's book—one which John is known to use, it may be a borrowed one, but generally known as some way connected with him,—Rev. Mr. Smith's church, St. John's church, Grace church, Murray's grammar; not the property nor in the possession of Lindley Murray, neither does it *govern him*; for he has gone to speak a purer language than he taught on earth. It is mine. I bought it, have possessed it these ten years; but, thank fortune, am little *governed* by it. But more on this point when we come to the proper place. What I have said, will serve as a hint, which will enable you to see the impropriety of adopting the "possessive case."

It may be said that more cases are employed in other languages. That is a poor reason why we should break the barriers of natural language. Beside, I know not how we should decide by that rule, for none of them have a *case* that will compare with the English possessive. The genitive of the French, Latin, or Greek, will apply in only a few respects. The former has *three*, the latter five, and the Latin six cases, neither of which correspond with the possessive, as explained by Murray and his satellites. We should be slow to adopt into our language an idiom which does not belong to it, and compel learners to make distinctions where none exist. It is an easy matter to tell children that the apostrophe and letter *s* marks the possessive case; but when they ask the difference in the meaning between the use of the noun and those which all admit are adjectives, it will be no indifferent task to satisfy them. What is the difference in the construction of language or the sense conveyed, between Hudson'*s* river, and *Hudson* river? Davis's straits, or Bass straits? St. John's church, or Episcopal church? the sun's beams, or sun shine? In all cases these words are used to define the succeeding noun. They regard "property or possession," only when attending circumstances, altogether foreign from any quality in the form or meaning of the word itself, are so combined as to give it that import. And in such cases, we retain these words as adjectives, long after the property has passed from the hands of the persons who gave it a name. *Field's* point, *Fuller's* rocks, *Fisher's* island, *Fulton's* invention, will long be retained after those whose names were given to distinguish these things, have slept with their fathers and been forgotten. Blannerhassett's Island, long since ceased to be his property or tranquil possession, by confiscation; but it will retain its specific name, till the inundations of the Ohio's waters shall have washed it away and left not a wreck behind.

The distinctions I have made in the positions of nouns, will be clearly understood when we come to the verbs. A few remarks upon pronouns will close the present lecture.

PRONOUNS.

Pronouns are such as the word indicates. *Pro* is the latin word *for*; pro-nomen, *for nouns*. They are words, originally nouns, used specifically *for* other nouns, to avoid the too frequent repetition of the same words; as, Washington was the father of his country; *he* was a valiant officer. *We* ought to respect *him*. The word *we*, stands for the speaker and all present, and saves the trouble of naming them; *he* and *him*, stand for Washington, to avoid the monotony which would be produced by a recurrence of his name.

Pronouns are all of one kind, and few in number. I will give you a list of them in their respective positions.

					Agents.	Objects.
	1st	person,			I,	me,
	2d	"			thou,	thee,
Singular	3d	"	mas.	he,		him,
		"	fem.	she,		her,
				it,		it.
	1st	person,			we,	us,
Plural	2d	"			ye, or you,	you,
	3d	"			they,	them,
					who,	whom.

The two last may be used in either person, number, or gender.

The frequent use of these words render them very important, in the elegant and rapid use of language. They are so short, and their sound so soft and easy, that the frequency of their recurrence does not mar the beauty of a sentence, but saves us from the redundancy of other words. They are substituted only when there is little danger of mistaking the nouns for which they stand. They are, however, sometimes used in a very broad sense; as, "*they say* it is so;" meaning no particular persons, but the general sentiment. *It* frequently takes the lead of a sentence, and the thing represented by it comes after; as, "It is currently reported, that things were thus and so." Here *it* represents the single idea which is afterward stated at length. "*It* is so." "*It* may be that the nations will be destroyed by wars, earthquakes, and famines." But more of this when we come to speak of the composition of sentences.

The words now classed as pronouns were originally *names* of things, but in this character they have long been obsolete. They are now used only in their secondary character as the representatives of other words. The word *he*, for instance, signified originally *to breathe*. It was applied to the living beings who inhaled air. It occurs with little change in the various languages of Europe, ancient and modern, till at length it is applied to the male agent which lives and acts. The word *her* means *light*, but is specifically applied to females which are the objects of action.

Was it in accordance with the design of these lectures, it would give me pleasure to go into a minute examination of the origin, changes and meaning of these words till they came to be applied as specific words of exceeding limited character. Most of them might be traced thro all the languages of Europe; the Arabic, Persic, Arminian, Chaldean, Hebrew, and, for ought I know, all the languages of Asia. But as they are now admitted a peculiar position in the expression of thought from which they never vary; and as we are contending about philosophic principles rather than verbal criticisms, I shall forbear a further consideration of these words.

In the proper place I shall consider those words formerly called "Adjective Pronouns," "Pronoun Adjectives," or "Pronominal Adjectives," to suit the varying whims of those grammar makers, who desired to show off a speck of improvement in their "simplifying" works without ever having a new idea to express. It is a query in some minds whether the seventy-two "simplifiers" and "improvers" of Murray's grammar ever had any distinct notions in their heads which they did not obtain from the very man, who, it would seem by their conduct, was unable to explain his own meaning.

LECTURE VI.

ON ADJECTIVES.

Definition of adjectives. — General character. — Derivation. — How understood. — Defining and describing. — Meaning changes to suit the noun. — Too numerous. — Derived from nouns. — Nouns and verbs made from adjectives. — Foreign adjectives. — A general list. — Difficult to be understood. — An example. — Often superfluous. — Derived from verbs. — Participles. — Some prepositions. — Meaning unknown. — With. — In. — Out. — Of.

The most important sub-division of words is the class called Adjectives, which we propose to notice this evening. *Adjective* signifies *added* or *joined to*. We employ the term in grammar to designate that class of words which are *added to nouns to define or describe them*. In doing this, we strictly adhere to the principles we have already advanced, and do not deviate from the laws of nature, as developed in the regulation of speech.

In speaking of things, we had occasion to observe that the mind not only conceived ideas of things, but of their properties; as, the hardness of flint; the heat of fire; and that we spoke of one thing in reference to another. We come now to consider this subject more at large.

In the use of language the mind first rests on the thing which is present before it, or the word which represents the idea of that thing. Next it observes the changes and attitudes of these things. Thirdly, it conceives ideas of their qualities and relations to other things. The first use of these words is to name things. This we call *nouns*. The second is to express their actions. This we call *verbs*. The last is to define or describe things. This we call *adjectives*. There is a great similarity between the words used to name things and to express their actions; as, builders build buildings; singers sing songs; writers write writings; painters paint paintings. In the popular use of language we vary these words to avoid the monotony and give pleasantness and variety. We say builders *erect* houses, barns, and other buildings; singers perform pieces of music; musicians play tunes; the choir sing psalm tunes; artists paint pictures.

From these two classes a third is derived which partakes somewhat of the nature of both, and yet from its secondary use, it has obtained a distinctive character, and as such is allowed a separate position among the classes of words.

It might perhaps appear more in order to pass the consideration of adjectives till we have noticed the character and use of verbs, from which an important portion of them is derived. But as they are used in connexion with nouns, and as the character they borrow from the verb will be readily understood, I have preferred to retain the old arrangement, and consider them in this place.

Adjectives are words added to nouns to define or describe them. They are derived either, 1st, from nouns; as, *window* glass, *glass* window, a stone house, building stone, maple sugar, sugar cane; or, 2d, from verbs; as, a *written* paper, a *printed* book, a *painted* house, a *writing* desk. In the first case we employ one noun, or the name of one thing, to define another, thus giving it a secondary use. A *glass* window is one made of glass, and not of any thing else. It is neither a *board* window, nor a *paper* window. *Maple* sugar is not *cane* sugar, nor *beet* sugar, nor *molasses* sugar; but it may be *brown* sugar, if it has been browned, or *white* if it has been whit*ed* or whit*ened*. In this case, you at once perceive the correctness of our second proposition, in the derivation of adjectives from verbs, by which we describe a thing in reference to its condition, in some way affected by the operation of a prior action. A *printed* book is one on which the action of printing has been performed. A *written* book differs from the former, in as much as its appearance was produced by writing and not by printing.

In the definition or description of things, whatever is best understood is employed as a definitive or descriptive term, and is attached to the object to make known its properties and relations. Speaking of nations, if we desire to distinguish some from others, we choose the words supposed to be best known, and talk of European, African, American, or Indian nations;

northern, southern, eastern, or western nations. These last words are used in reference to their relative position, and may be variously understood; for we speak of the northern, eastern, western, and southern nations of Europe, of Africa, and the world.

Again, we read of civiliz*ed*, half-civilized, and barbarous nations; learned, unlearned, ignorant, and enlightened; rich, powerful, enterprising, respected, ancient or modern, christian, mahomedan or pagan. In these, and a thousand similar cases, we decide the meaning, not alone from the word employed as an adjective, but from the subject of remark; for, were we to attach the same meaning to the same word, wherever used, we could not receive correct or definite impressions from the language of others—our inferences would be the most monstrous. A *great* mountain and a *great* pin, a *great* continent and a *great* farm, a *great* ocean and a *great* pond, a *great* grammar and a *great* scholar, refer to things of very different dimensions and character; or, as Mr. Murray would say, "*qualities.*" A mountain is great by comparison with other mountains; and a pin, compared with other pins, may be very large—exceeding great—and yet fall very far short of the size of a very small mountain. A *small* man may be a *great* scholar, and a rich neighbor a poor friend. A sweet flower is often very bitter to the taste. A *good* horse would make a *bad* dinner, but *false* grammar can never make *true* philologists.

All words are to be understood according to their use. Their meaning can be determined in no other way. Many words change their forms to express their relations, but fewer in our language than in most others, ancient or modern. Other words remain the same, or nearly so, in every position; noun, adjective, or verb, agent or object, past or present. To determine whether a word is an adjective, first ascertain whether it names a thing, defines or describes it, or expresses its action, and you will never be at a loss to know to what class it belongs.

The business of adjectives is twofold, and they may be distinguished by the appellations of *defining* or *describing* adjectives. This distinction is in many cases unimportant; in others it is quite essential. The same word in one case may *define*, in others *describe* the object, and occasionally do both, for we often specify things by their descriptions. The learner has only to ascertain the meaning and use of the adjective to decide whether it defines or describes the subject of remark. If it is employed to distinguish one thing from the general mass, or one class from other classes, it has the former character; but after such thing is pointed out, if it is used to give a description of its character or properties, its character is different, and should be so understood and explained.

Defining adjectives are used to *point out*, specify or distinguish certain things from others of their kind, or one sort from other sorts, and answer to the questions *which, what, how many,* or *how much.*

Describing adjectives express the character and qualities of things, and give a more full and distinct knowledge than was before possessed.

In a case before mentioned, we spoke of the "Indian nations." The word *Indian* was chosen to specify or define what nations were alluded to. But all may not decide alike in this case. Some may think we meant the aborigines of America; others, that the southern nations of Asia were referred to. This difficulty originates in a misapprehension of the definitive word chosen. India was early known as the name of the south part of Asia, and the people there, were called Indians. When Columbus discovered the new world, supposing he had reached the country of India, which had long been sought by a voyage round the coast of Africa, he named it India, and the people Indians. But when the mistake was discovered, and the truth fully known, instead of effecting a change in the name already very generally understood, and in common use, another word was chosen to distinguish between countries so opposite and *West* India became the word to distinguish the newly discovered islands; and as India was little better known in Europe at that time, instead of retaining their old name unaltered, another word was prefixed, and they called it *East* India. When, therefore, we desire to be definite, we retain these words, and say, East Indians and West Indians. Without this distinction, we should understand the native people of our own country; but in Europe, Asia, and Africa, they would think we alluded to those in Asia. So with all other adjectives which are not understood. *Indian,* as an adjective, may also be employed to *describe* the character and condition of the aborigines. We talk of an indian temper, indian looks, indian blankets, furs, &c.

In writing and conversation we should employ words to explain, to define and describe, which are better understood than those things of which we speak. The pedantry of some modern writers in this respect is ridiculous. Not satisfied to use plain terms which every body can understand, they hunt the dictionaries from alpha to omega, and not unfrequently overleap the "king's english," and ransack other languages to find an unheard of word, or a list of adjectives never before arranged together, in so nice a manner, so that their ideas are lost to the common reader, if not to themselves. This fault may be alleged against too many of our public speakers, as well as the affected gentry of the land. They are like Shakspeare's Gratiano, "who speaks an infinite deal of nothing, more than any man in all Venice; his reasons are as two grains of wheat hid in two bushels of chaff: you shall seek all day ere you find them; and, when you have found them, they are not worth the search." Such sentences remind us of the painting of the young artist who drew the form of an animal, but apprehensive that some might mistake it, wrote under it, "*This is a horse.*"

In forming our notions of what is signified by an adjective, the mind should pause to determine the meaning of such word when used as a distinct name for some object, in order to determine the import of it in this new capacity. A *tallow* candle is one made of a substance called tallow, and is employed to distinguish it from wax or spermaceti candles. The adjective in this case, names the article of which the candle is made, and is thus a noun, but, as we are not speaking of tallow, but of candles, we place it in a new relation, and give it a new grammatical character. But you will perceive the correctness of a former assertion, that all words may be reduced to two classes, and that adjectives are derived from nouns or verbs.

But you may inquire if there are not some adjectives in use which have no corresponding verb or noun from which they are derived. There are many words in our language which in certain uses have become obsolete, but are retained in others. We now use some words as verbs which originally were known only as nouns, and others as nouns which are unknown as verbs. We also put a new construction upon words and make nouns, verbs and adjectives promiscuously and with little regard to rule or propriety. Words at one time unknown become familiar by use, and others are laid aside for those more new or fashionable. These facts are so obvious that I shall be excused from extending my remarks to any great length. But I will give an example which will serve as a clew to the whole. Take the word *happy*, long known only as an adjective. Instead of following this word *back* to its primitive use and deriving it directly from its noun, or as a past participle, such as it is in truth, we have gone *forward* and made from it the noun *happiness*, and, in more modern days, are using the verb *happify*, a word, by the way, in common use, but which has not yet been honored with a place in our dictionaries; altho Mr. Webster has given us, as he says, the *unauthorised* (un-author-ised) word "happifying." Perhaps he had never heard or read some of our greatest savans, who, if not the authors, employ the word *happify* very frequently in the pulpit and halls of legislation, and at the bar, as well as in common parlance.

Happy is the past participle of the verb *to hap*, or, as afterwards used, with a nice shade of change in the meaning, *to happen*. It means *happied*, or made happy by those favorable circumstances which have *happened* to us. Whoever will read our old writers no further back than Shakspeare, will at once see the use and changes of this word. They will find it in all its forms, simple and compound, as a verb, noun, and adjective. "It may *hap* that he will come." It happened as I was going that I found my lost child, and was thereby made quite happy. The man desired to *hap*pify himself and family without much labor, so he engaged in speculation; and *hap*pily he was not so *hap*less in his pursuit of *hap*piness as often *hap*pens to such *hap*-hazard fellows, for he soon became very *hap*py with a moderate fortune.

But to the question. There are many adjectives in our language which are borrowed from foreign words. Instead of *adjectiving* our own nouns we go to our neighbors and *adjective* and anglicise [english-ise] their words, and adopt the pampered urchins into our own family and call them our favorites. It is no wonder that they often appear aukward and unfamiliar, and that our children are slow in forming an intimate acquaintance with them. You are here favored with a short list of these words which will serve as examples, and enable you to comprehend my meaning and apply it in future use. Some of them are regularly used as adjectives, with or without change; others are not.

ENGLISH NOUNS.	FOREIGN ADJECTIVES.
Alone	Sole, solitary
Alms	Eleemosynary

Age	Primeval
Belief	Credulous
Blame	Culpable
Breast	Pectoral
Being	Essential
Bosom	Graminal, sinuous
Boy, boyish	Puerile
Blood, bloody	Sanguinary, sanguine
Burden	Onerous
Beginning	Initial
Boundary	Conterminous
Brother	Fraternal
Bowels	Visceral
Body	Corporeal
Birth	Natal, native
Calf	Vituline
Carcass	Cadaverous
Cat	Feline
Cow	Vaccine
Country	Rural, rustic
Church	Ecclesiastical
Death	Mortal
Dog	Canine
Day	Diurnal, meridian, ephemeral
Disease	Morbid
East	Oriental
Egg	Oval
Ear	Auricular
Eye	Ocular
Flesh	Carnal, carnivorous
Father	Paternal
Field	Agrarian

Flock	Gregarious
Foe	Hostile
Fear	Timorous, timid
Finger	Digital
Flattery	Adulatory
Fire	Igneous
Faith	Fiducial
Foot	Pedal
Groin	Inguinal
Guardian	Tutelar
Glass	Vitreous
Grape	Uveous
Grief	Dolorous
Gain	Lucrative
Help	Auxiliary
Heart	Cordial, cardiac
Hire	Stipendiary
Hurt	Noxious
Hatred	Odious
Health	Salutary, salubrious
Head	Capital, chief
Ice	Glacial
Island	Insular
King	Regal, royal
Kitchen	Culinary
Life	Vital, vivid, vivarious
Lungs	Pulmonary
Lip	Labial
Leg	Crural, isosceles
Light	Lucid, luminous
Love	Amorous
Lust	Libidinous

Law	Legal, loyal
Mother	Maternal
Money	Pecuniary
Mixture	Promiscuous, miscellaneous
Moon	Lunar, sublunary
Mouth	Oral
Marrow	Medulary
Mind	Mental
Man	Virile, male, human, masculine
Milk	Lacteal
Meal	Ferinaceous
Nose	Nasal
Navel	Umbilical
Night	Nocturnal, equinoctial
Noise	Obstreperous
One	First
Parish	Parochial
People	Popular, populous, public, epidemical, endemical
Point	Punctual
Pride	Superb, haughty
Plenty	Copious
Pitch	Bituminous
Priest	Sacerdotal
Rival	Emulous
Root	Radical
Ring	Annular
Reason	Rational
Revenge	Vindictive
Rule	Regular
Speech	Loquacious, garrulous, eloquent
Smell	Olfactory
Sight	Visual, optic, perspicuous, conspicuous

Side	Lateral, collateral
Skin	Cutaneous
Spittle	Salivial
Shoulder	Humeral
Shepherd	Pastoral
Sea	Marine, maritime
Share	Literal
Sun	Solar
Star	Astral, sideral, stellar
Sunday	Dominical
Spring	Vernal
Summer	Estival
Seed	Seminal
Ship	Naval, nautical
Shell	Testaceous
Sleep	Soporiferous
Strength	Robust
Sweat	Sudorific
Step	Gradual
Sole	Venal
Two	Second
Treaty	Federal
Trifle	Nugatory
Tax	Fiscal
Time	Temporal, chronical
Town	Oppidan
Thanks	Gratuitous
Theft	Furtive
Threat	Minatory
Treachery	Insidious
Thing	Real
Throat	Jugular, gutteral

Taste	Insipid
Thought	Pensive
Thigh	Femoral
Tooth	Dental
Tear	Lachrymal
Vessel	Vascular
World	Mundane
Wood	Sylvan, savage
Way	Devious, obvious, impervious, trivial
Worm	Vermicular
Whale	Cutaceous
Wife	Uxorious
Word	Verbal, verbose
Weak	Hebdomadal
Wall	Mural
Will	Voluntary, spontaneous
Winter	Brumal
Wound	Vulnerary
West	Occidental
War	Martial
Women	Feminine, female, effeminate
Year	Annual, anniversary, perennial, triennial

Such are some of the adjectives introduced into our language from other nations. The list will enable you to discover that when we have no adjective of our own to correspond with the noun, we borrow from our neighbors an adjective derived from one of their nouns, to which we give an english termination. For example:

English Noun.	Latin Noun.	Adjective.
Boy	Puer	Puerile
Grief	Dolor	Dolorous
Thought	Pensa	Pensive

Wife	Uxor	Uxorious
Word	Verbum	Verbal, verbose
Year	Annum	Annual
Body	Corpus	Corporeal
Head	Caput	Capital
Church	Ekklesia (*Greek*)	Ecclesiastical
King	Roi (*French*)	Royal
Law	Loi "	Loyal

It is exceedingly difficult to understand the adjectives of many nouns with which we are familiar, from the fact above stated, that they are derived from other languages, and not our own. The most thoro scholars have found this task no easy affair. Most grammarians have let it pass unobserved; but every person has seen the necessity of some explanation upon this point, to afford a means of ascertaining the etymological derivation and meaning of these words. I would here enter farther into this subject, but I am reminded that I am surpassing the limits set me for this course of lectures.

The attention I have bestowed on this part of the present subject, will not be construed into a mere verbal criticism. It has been adopted to show you how, in the definition or description of things, the mind clings to one thing to gain some information concerning another. When we find a thing unlike any thing else we have ever known, in form, in size, in color, in every thing; we should find it a difficult task, if not an impossibility, to describe it to another in a way to give any correct idea of it. Having never seen its like before, we can say little of its character. We may give it a *name*, but that would not be understood. We could say it was as large as—no, it had no size; that it was like—but no, it had no likeness; that it resembled—no, it had no resemblance. How could we describe it? What could we say of it? Nothing at all.

What idea could the Pacha of Egypt form of ice, having never seen any till the french chemists succeeded in freezing water in his presence? They told him of ice; that it was *cold*; that it would freeze; that whole streams were often frozen over, so that men and teams could walk over them. He believed no such thing—it was a "christian lie." This idea was confirmed on the first trial of the chemists, which failed of success. But when, on the second attempt, they succeeded, he was all in raptures. A new field was open before him. New ideas were produced in his mind. New qualities were learned; and he could now form some idea of the *ice* bergs of the north; of *frozen* regions, which he had never seen; of *icy* hearts, and storms of *frozen* rain.

We often hear it said, such a man is very *stoical*; another is an *epicurean*; and another is a *bacchanal*, or *bacchanalian*. But what idea should we form of such persons, if we had never read of the Stoics and their philosophy; of Epicurus and his notions of happiness and duty; or of Bacchus, the god of wine and revelry, whose annual feasts, or Dionysia, were celebrated with the most extravagant licentiousness thro out Greece and Rome, till put down by the Senate of the latter.

You can not fail to see the importance of the knowledge on which we here insist. The meaning you attach to words is exceedingly diverse; and hence you are not always able to think alike, or understand each other, nor derive the same sentiment from the same language. The contradictory opinions which exist in the world may be accounted for, in a great measure, in this way. Our knowledge of many things of which we speak, is limited, either from lack of means, or disposition to employ them. People always differ and contend most about things of which they know the least. Did we all attach the same meaning to the same words, our opinions would all be the same, as true as the forty-fifth problem of Euclid. How important, then, that children should always be taught the same meaning of words, and learn to use them correctly. Etymology, viewed in this light, is a most important branch of science.

Whenever a word is sufficiently understood, no adjective should be connected with it. There is a ridiculous practice among many people, of appending to every noun one or more adjectives, which have no other effect than to expose their own folly. Some writers are so in the habit of annexing adjectives to all nouns, that they dare not use one without. You will not unfrequently see adjectives different in form, added to a noun of very similar meaning; as, sad melancholy, an ominous sign, this mundane earth, pensive thoughts.

When words can be obtained, which not only name the object, but also describe its properties, it should be preferred to a noun with an adjective; as *pirate*, for *sea robber*; *savan*, for a *learned* or *wise man*.[4]

In relation to that class of adjectives derived from verbs, we will be brief. They include what have been termed participles, not a distinct "part of speech," but by some included in the verbs. We use them as adjectives to describe things as standing in some relation to other things on the account of the action expressed by the verb from which they are derived. "The man is respected." *Respected*, in this case, describes the man in such a relation to those who have become acquainted with his good qualities, that he now receives their respect. He is respect*able*, (*able* to command, or worthy of respect,) and of course, respected for his respectability. To avoid repetition, we select different words to assist in the expression of a complex idea. But I indulge in phrases like the above, to show the nice shades of meaning in the common use of words, endeavoring to analyze, as far as possible, our words and thoughts, and show their mutual connexion and dependencies.

What has been termed the "present participle" is also an adjective, describing things in their present condition in reference to actions. "The man is writing." Here, *writing* describes the man in his present employment. But the consideration of this matter more properly belongs to the construction of sentences.

———————————

There is another class or variety of words properly belonging to this division of grammar, which may as well be noticed in this place as any other. I allude to those words generally called "Prepositions." We have not time now to consider them at large, but will give you a brief view of our opinion of them, and reserve the remainder of our remarks till we come to another part of these lectures.

Most of the words called prepositions, in books of grammar, are participles, derived from verbs, many of which are still in use, but some are obsolete. They are used in the true character of adjectives, *describing one thing by its relation to another*. But their meaning has not been generally understood. Our dictionaries have afforded no means by which we can trace their etymology. They have been regarded as a kind of cement to stick other words together, having no meaning or importance in themselves.[5] Until their meaning is known, we can not reasonably expect to draw them from their hiding places, and give them a respectable standing in the transmission of thought.

Many words, from the frequency of their use, fail to attract our attention as much as those less employed; not because they are less important, but because they are so familiarly known that the operations of thought are not observed in the choice made of them to express ideas. If we use words of which little is known, we ponder well before we adopt them, to determine whether the sense usually attached to them accords exactly with the notions we desire to convey by them. The same can not be said of small words which make up a large proportion of our language, and are, in fact, more necessary than the others, in as much as their meaning is more generally known. Those who employ carriages to convey their bodies, observe little of their construction, unless there is something singular or fine in their appearance. The common parts are unobserved, yet as important as the small words used in the common construction of language, the vehicle of thought. As the apostle says of the body politic, "those members of the body, which seem to be more feeble, are necessary;" so the words least understood by grammarians are most necessary in the correct formation of language.

It is an easy matter to get along with the words called prepositions, after they are all learned by rote; but when their meaning and use are inquired into, the best grammarians have little to say of them.

A list of prepositions, alphabetically arranged, is found in nearly every grammar, which scholars are required to commit to memory, without knowing any thing of their meaning or use, only that they are prepositions when an objective word comes after them, *because the books say so*; but occasionally the same words occur as adverbs and adjectives. There is, however, no trouble in "parsing" them, unless the list is forgotten. In that case, you will see the pupil, instead of inquiring after the meaning and duty of the word, go to the book and search for it in the lists of prepositions or conjunctions; or to the dictionary, to see if there is a "*prep.*" appended to it. What will children ever learn of language in this way? Of what avail is all such grammar teaching? As soon as they leave school it is all forgotten; and you will hear them say, at the very time they should be reaping the harvest of former toil, that they once understood grammar, but it is all gone from them. Poor souls! their memory is very treacherous, else they have never learned language as they ought. There is a fault somewhere. To us it is not difficult to determine where it is.

That certain words are prepositions, there can be no doubt, because the books say they are; but *why* they are so, is quite another matter. All we desire is to have their meaning understood. Little difficulty will then be found in determining their use.

I have said they are derived from verbs, many of which are obsolete. Some are still in use, both as verbs and nouns. Take for example the word WITH. This word signifies *joined* or *united*. It is used to show that two things are some how joined together so that they are spoke of in connexion. It frequently occurs in common conversation, as a verb and noun, but not as frequently in the books as formerly. The farmer says to his *hired* man, "Go and get a *withe* and come and *withe* up the fence;" that is, get some pliant twigs of tough wood, twist them together, and *withe* or bind them round these posts, so that one may stand firm *with*, or *withed* to, the other. A book *with* a cover, is one that has a cover *joined*, bound, or attached to it. "A father *with* a son, a man *with* an estate, a nation *with* a constitution." In all such cases *with* expresses the relation between the two things mentioned, produced by a *union* or connexion with each other.[6]

IN is used in the same way. It is still retained as a noun and is suspended on the signs of many public houses. "The traveller's *inn*," is a house where travellers *in* themselves, or go *in*, for entertainment. It occurs frequently in Shakspeare and in more modern writers, as a verb, and is still used in common conversation as an imperative. "Go, *in* the crops of grain." "*In* with you." "*In* with it." In describes one thing by its relation to another, which is the business of adjectives. It admits of the regular degrees of comparison; as, *in*, *inner*, *innermost* or *inmost*. It also has its compounds. *In*step, the *inner* part of the foot, *in*let, *in*vestment, *in*heritance. In this capacity it is extensively used under its different shades of meaning which I cannot stop to notice.

OF signifies *divided, separated,* or *parted.* "The ship is *off* the coast." "I am bound *off,* and you are bound *out.*" "A part *of* a pencil," is that part which is *separated* from the rest, implying that the act of *separating,* or *offing,* has taken place. "A branch *of* the tree." There is the tree; this branch is from it. "Our communication was broken *off* several years ago." "Sailors record their *off*ings, and parents love their *off*spring," or those children which sprung from them.[7] "We also *are his offspring;*" that is, sprung from God. [8] In all these, and every other case, you will perceive the meaning of the word, and its office will soon appear essential in the expression of thought. Had all the world been a compact whole, nothing ever separated from it, we could never speak of a part *of* it, for we could never have such an idea. But we look at things, as separated, divided, parted; and speak of one thing as separated from the others. Hence, when we speak of the part of the earth we inhabit, we, in imagination, separate it from some other *part,* or the general whole. We can not use this word in reference to a thing which is indivisible, because we can conceive no idea of a part *of* an indivisible thing. We do not say, a portion *of* our mind taken as a whole, but as capable of division. A share *of* our regards, supposes that the remainder is reserved for something else.

OUT, out*er* or utter, outer*most* or utmost, admits of the same remark as *in.*

In this manner, we might explain a long list of words, called adverbs, conjunctions, and prepositions. But I forbear, for the present, the further consideration of this subject, and leave it for another lecture.

We resume the consideration of Adjectives. The importance of this class of words in the expression of our thoughts, is my excuse for bestowing upon it so much labor. Had words always been used according to their primitive meaning, there would be little danger of being misunderstood. But the fact long known, "*Verba mutanter*"—words change—has been the prolific source of much of the diversity of opinion, asperity of feeling, and apparent misconstruction of other's sentiments, which has disturbed society, and disgraced mankind. I have, in a former lecture, alluded to this point, and call it up in this place to prepare your minds to understand what is to be said on the secondary use of words in the character of adjectives.

I have already spoken of adjectives in general, as derived from nouns and verbs, and was somewhat particular upon the class sometimes called *prepositions*, which describe one thing by its relation to another, produced by some action which has placed them in such relation. We will now pass to examine a little more minutely into the character and use of certain adjectives, and the manner of their derivation.

We commence with those derived from nouns, both common and proper, which are somewhat peculiar in their character. I wish you distinctly to bear in mind the use of adjectives. They are words *added to nouns to define or describe them.*

Many words which name things, are used as adjectives, with out change; as, *ox* beef, *beef* cattle, *paper* books, *straw* hats, *bonnet* paper. Others admit of change, or addition; as, natio*nal* character, a merci*ful* (mercy-*ful*) man, a gloom*y* prospect, a fam*ous* horse, a gold*en* ball. The syllables which are added, are parts of words, which are at first compounded with them, till, by frequency of use, they are incorporated into the same word. "A merci*ful* man" is one who is full of mercy. A gold*en* ball is one made of gold. This word is sometimes used without change; as, a *gold* ring.

A numerous portion of these words take the syllable *ly*, contracted from *like*, which is still retained in many words; as, Judas-*like*, lady-*like*, gentleman-*like*. These two last words, are of late, occasionally used as other words, lady*ly*, gentleman*ly*; but the last more frequently than the former. She behaved very ladi*ly*, or lady*like*; and his appearance was quite gentleman*ly*. But to say ladi*ly* appearance, does not yet sound quite soft enough; but it is incorrect only because it is uncommon. God*ly* and god*like* are both in use, and equally correct, with a nice shade of difference in meaning.

All grammarians have found a difficulty in the word *like*, which they were unable to unravel. They could never account for its use in expressing a relation between two objectives. They forgot that to be like, one thing must be *likened* to another, and that it was the very meaning of this word to express such lik*eness*. John looks *like* his brother. The looks, the countenance, or appearance of John, are *likened* to his brother's looks or appearance. "This machine is more like the pattern than any I have seen." Here the adjective *like* takes the comparative degree, as it is called, to show a nearer resemblance than has been before observed between the things compared. "He has a statesman-*like* appearance." I *like* this apple, because it agrees with my taste; it has qualities *like* my notion of what is palateable." In every situation the word is used to express likeness between two things. It describes one thing by its likeness to another.

Many adjectives are formed from proper nouns by adding an apostrophe and the letter *s*, except when the word ends in *s*, in which case the final *s* is usually omitted for the sake of euphony. This, however, was not generally adopted by old writers. It is not observed in the earliest translations of the Bible into the english language. It is now in common practice. Thus, Montgomery's monument in front of St. Paul's church; Washington's funeral; Shay's rebelion; England's bitterest foes; Hamlet's father's ghost; Peter's wife's mother; Todd's, Walker's, Johnson's dictionary; Winchell's Watts' hymns; Pond's Murray's grammar. No body would suppose that the "relation of property or possession" was expressed in these cases, as our grammar books tell us, but that the terms employed are used to *define* certain objects, about which we are speaking. They possess the true character and use of adjectives, and as such let them be regarded. It must be as false as frivolous to say that Montgomery, who nobly fell at the siege of Quebec, *owns* the monument erected over his remains, which were conveyed to New-York many years after his death; or that St. Paul *owns* or *possesses* the church beneath which they were deposited; that Hamlet owned his father, and his father his ghost; that Todd owns Walker, and Walker owns Johnson, and Johnson his dictionary which may have had a hundred owners, and never been the property of its author, but printed fifty years after his death. These words, I repeat, are merely *definitive* terms, and like others serve to point out or specify particular objects which may thus be better known.

Words, however, in common use form adjectives the same as other words; as, Russia iron, China ships, India silks, Vermont cheese, Orange county butter, New-York flour, Carolina potatoes. Morocco leather was first manufactured in a city of Africa called by that name, but it is now made in almost every town in our country. The same may be said of Leghorn hats, Russia binding, French shoes, and China ware. Although made in our own country we still retain the words, morocco, leghorn, russia, french, and china, to define the fashion, kind, or quality of articles to which we allude. Much china ware is made in Liverpool, which, to distinguish it from the real, is called liverpool china. Many french shoes are made in Lynn, and many Roxbury russets, Newton pippins, and Rhode-Island greenings, grow in Vermont.

It may not be improper here to notice the adjectives derived from pronouns, which retain so much of their character as relates to the persons who employ them. These are *my, thy, his, her, its, our, your, their, whose*. This is *my* book, that is *your* pen, this is *his* knife, and that is *her* letter. Some of these, like other words, vary their ending when standing alone; as, two apples are your*s*, three her*s*, six their*s*, five our*s*, and the rest mine. *His* does not alter in popular use. Hence the reason why you hear it so often, in common conversation, when standing without the noun expressed, pronounced as if written *hisen*. The word *other*, and some others, come under the same remark. When the nouns specified are expressed, they take the regular termination; as, give me these Baldwin apples, and a few others —a few other apples.

There is a class of small words which from the frequency of their use have, like pronouns, lost their primitive character, and are now preserved only as adjectives. Let us examine a few of them by endeavoring to ferret out their true meaning and application in the expression of ideas. We will begin with the old articles, *a*, *an*, and *the*, by testing the truth and propriety of the duty commonly assigned to them in our grammars.

The standard grammar asserts that "an article is a word prefixed to substantives, to point them out, and to show how far their signification extends; as, "a garden, an eagle, the woman." Skepticism in grammar is no crime, so we will not hesitate to call in question the correctness of this "best of all grammars beyond all comparison." Let us consider the very examples given. They were doubtless the best that could be found. Does *a* "point out" the garden, or "show how far its signification extends?" It does neither of these things. It may name "*any*" garden, and it certainly does not define whether it is a *great* or a *small* one. It simply determines that *one* garden is the subject of remark. All else is to be determined by the word *garden*.

We are told there are two articles, the one *in*definite, the other definite—*a* is the former, and *the* the latter. I shall leave it with you to reconcile the apparent contradiction of an *indefinite* article which "is used in a *vague sense, to point out the signification* of another word." But I challenge teachers to make their pupils comprehend such a jargon, if they can do it themselves. But it is as good sense as we find in many of the popular grammars of the day.

Again, Murray says "*a* becomes *an* before a vowel or silent *h*;" and so say all his *simplifying* satellites after him. Is such the fact? Is he right? He is, I most unqualifiedly admit, with this little correction, the addition of a single word—he is right *wrong*! Instead of *a* becoming *an*, the reverse is the fact. The word is derived directly from the same word which still stands as our first numeral. It was a short time since written *ane*, as any one may see by consulting all old books. By and by it dropped the *e*, and afterwards, for the sake of euphony, in certain cases, the *n*, so that now it stands a single letter. You all have lived long enough to have noticed the changes in the word. Formerly we said *an* union, *an* holiday, *an* universalist, *an* unitarian, &c., expressions which are now rarely heard. We now say *a* union, &c. This single instance proves that arbitrary rules of grammar have little to do in the regulation of language. Its barriers are of sand, soon removed. It will not be said that this is an unimportant mistake, for, if an error, it is pernicious, and if a grammarian knows enough to say that *a* becomes *an*, he ought to know that he tells a falsehood, and that *an* becomes *a* under certain circumstances. Mr. Murray gives the following example to illustrate the use of *a*. "Give me *a* book; that is, *any* book." How can the learner understand such a rule? How will it apply? Let us try it. "A man has *a* wife;" that is, *any* man has *any* wife. I have a hat; that is, *any* hat. A farmer has a farm—*any* farmer has *any* farm. A merchant in Boston has a beautiful piece of broadcloth—*any* merchant in Boston has any beautiful piece of broadcloth. A certain king of Europe decreed a protestant to be burned—*any* king of Europe decreed *any* protestant to be burned. How ridiculous are the rules we have learned and taught to others, to enable them to "speak and write with propriety." No wonder we never understood grammar, if so at variance with truth and every day's experience. The rules of grammar as usually taught can never be observed in practice. Hence it is called a *dry study*. In every thing else we learn something that we can understand, which will answer some good purpose in the affairs of life. But this branch of science is among the things which have been tediously learned to no purpose. No good account can be given of its advantages.

The, we are told, "is called the definite article, because it ascertains what *particular* thing or things are meant." A most unfortunate definition, and quite as erroneous as the former. Let us try it. *The* stars shine, *the* lion roars, *the* camel is a beast of burden, *the* deer is good for food, *the* wind blows, *the* clouds appear, *the* Indians are abused. What is there in these examples, which "ascertain what *particular* thing or things are meant?" They are expressions as *in*definite as we can imagine.

On the other hand, should I say *a* star shines, *a* lion roars, *an* Indian is abused, *a* wind blows, *a* cloud appears, you would understand me to allude very *definitely* to *one* "particular" object, as separate and distinguished from others of its kind.

But what is the wonderful peculiarity in the meaning and use of these two little words that makes them so unlike every thing else, as to demand a separate "part of speech?" You may be surprised when I tell you that there are other words in our language derived from the same source and possessed of the same meaning; but such is the fact, as will soon appear. Let us ask for the etymology of these important words. *A* signifies *one*, never more, never less. In this respect it is always *definite*. It is sometimes applied to a single thing, sometimes to a whole class of things, to a [one] man, or to a [one] hundred men. It may be traced thro other languages, ancient and modern, with little modification in spelling; Greek *eis*, ein; Latin *unus*; Armoric *unan*; Spanish and Italian *uno*; Portuguese *hum*; French *un*; German *ein*; Danish *een, en*; Dutch *een*; Swedish *en*; Saxon, *an, aen, one*— from which ours is directly derived—old English *ane*; and more modernly *one, an, a*. In all languages it defines a thing to be *one*, a united or congregated whole, and the word *one* may always be substituted without affecting the sense. From it is derived our word *once*, which signifies *oned, united, joined*, as we shall see when we come to speak of "contractions." In some languages *a* is styled an article, in others it is not. The Latin, for instance, has no article, and the Greek has no *indefinite*. But all languages have words which are like ours, pure adjectives, employed to specify certain things. The argument drawn from the fact that some other languages have *articles*, and therefore ours should, is fallacious. The Latin, which was surpassed for beauty of style or power in deliverance by few, if any others, never suffered from the lack of articles. Nor is there any reason why we should honor two small adjectives with that high rank to the exclusion of others quite as worthy.

The is always used as a definitive word, tho it is the least definite of the defining adjectives. In fact when we desire to "*ascertain particularly* what thing is meant," we select some more definite word. "Give me *the* books." Which? "Those with red covers, that in calf, and this in Russia binding." *The* nations are at peace. What nations? *Those* which were at war. You perceive how we employ words which are more definite, that is, better understood, to "*point out*" the object of conversation, especially when there is any doubt in the case. What occasion, then, is there to give these [the?] words a separate "part of speech," since in character they do not differ from others in the language?

We will notice another frivolous distinction made by Mr. Murray, merely to show how learned men may be mistaken, and the folly of trusting to special rules in the general application of words. He says, "Thou art *a* man," is a very general and *harmless* expression; but, thou art *the* man, (as Nathan said to David,) is an assertion capable of striking terror and remorse into the heart." The distinction in meaning here, on which he insists, attaches to the articles *a* and *the*. It is a sufficient refutation of this definition to make a counter statement. Suppose we say, "Murray is *the* best grammarian in the world; or, he is *a* fool, *a* knave, and *a* liar." Which, think you, would be considered the most *harmless* expression? Suppose it had been said to Aaron Burr, thou art *a* traitor, or to General William Hull, thou art *a* coward, would they regard the phrase as "*harmless!*" On the other hand, suppose a beautiful, accomplished, and talented young lady, should observe to one of her suitors, "I have received offers of marriage from several gentlemen besides yourself, but thou art THE man of my choice;" would it, think you, *strike* terror and remorse into his heart? I should pity the young student of Murray whose feelings had become so stoical from the false teaching of his author as to be filled with "terror and remorse" under such favorable circumstances, while fair prospects of future happiness were thus rapidly brightening before him. I speak as to the wise, judge ye what I say.

The adjective *that* has obtained a very extensive application in language. However, it may seem to vary in its different positions, it still retains its primitive meaning. It is comprised of *the* and *it*, thait, theat, thaet (Saxon,) thata (Gothic,) dat (Dutch.) It is the most decided definitive in our language. It is by use applied to things in the singular, or to a multitude of things regarded as a whole. By use, it applies to a collection of ideas expressed in a sentence; as, it was resolved, *that*. What? Then follows *that fact* which was resolved. "Provided *that*, in case he does" so and so. "It was agreed *that*," *that fact* was agreed to which is about to be made known. I wish you to understand, all thro these lectures, *that* I shall honestly endeavor to expose error and establish truth. Wish you to understand *what*? *that fact*, afterwards stated, "I shall endeavor," &c. You can not mistake my meaning: *that* would be impossible. What would be impossible? Why, to mistake my meaning.

You can not fail to observe the true character of this word called by our grammarians "adjective pronoun," "relative pronoun," and "conjunction." They did not think to look for its meaning. Had that (duty) been done, it would have stood forth in its true character, an important defining word.

The only difficulty in the explanation of this word, originates in the fact, that it was formerly applied to the plural as well as singular number. It is now applied to the singular only when referring directly to an object; as, *that man*. And it never should be used otherwise. But we often see phrases like this; "These are the men *that* rebeled." It should be, "these are the men *who* rebeled." This difficulty can not be overcome in existing grammars on any other ground. In modern writings, such instances are rare. *This* and *that* are applied to the singular; *these* and *those* to the plural.

WHAT is a compound of two original words, and often retains the meaning of both, when employed as a compound relative, "having in itself both the antecedent and the relative," as our authors tell us. But when it is dissected, it will readily enough be understood to be an adjective, defining things under particular relations.

But I shall weary your patience, I fear, if I stay longer in this place to examine the etymology of small words. I intended to have shown the meaning and use of many words included in the list of conjunctions, which are truly adjectives, such as *both, as, so, neither, and,* etc.; but I let them pass for the present, to be resumed under the head of contractions.

From the view we have given of this class of words, we are saved the tediousness of studying the grammatical distinctions made in the books, where no real distinctions exist. In character these words are like adjectives; their meaning, like the meaning of all other words, is peculiar to themselves. Let that be known, and there will be little difficulty in classing them. We need not confuse the learner with "adjective pronouns, possessive adjective pronouns, distributive adjective pronouns, demonstrative adjective pronouns, *indefinite* adjective pronouns," nor any other adjective pronouns, which can never be understood nor explained. Children will be slow to apprehend the propriety of a union of *adjectives* and *pronouns*, when told that the former is always used *with* a noun, and never *for* one; and the latter always *for* a noun, but never *with* one; and yet, that there is such a strange combination as a "*distributive or indefinite adjective pronoun*,"—"confusion worse confounded."

In the french language, the gender of adjectives is varied so as to agree with the nouns to which they belong. "Possessive pronouns," as they are called, come under the same rule, which proves them to be in character, and formation, adjectives; else the person using them must change gender. The father says, *ma* (feminine) *fille*, my daughter; and the mother, *mon* (masculine) *fils*, my son; the same as they would say, *bon pere*, good father; *bonne mere*, good mother; or, in Latin, *bonus pater*, or *bona mater*; or, in Spanish, *bueno padre, buena madre*. In the two last languages, as well as all others, where the adjectives vary the termination so as to agree with the noun, the same fact may be observed in reference to their "pronouns." If it is a fact that these words are *pronouns*, that is, stand for other *nouns*, then the father is *feminine*, and the mother is *masculine*; and whoever uses them in reference to the opposite sex must change gender to do so.

Describing adjectives admit of variation to express different degrees of comparison. The regular degrees have been reckoned three; positive, comparative, and superlative. These are usually marked by changing the termination. The *positive* is determined by a comparison with other things; as, a great house, a small book, compared with others of their kind. This is truly a comparative degree. The *comparative* adds *er*; as, a great*er* house, a small*er* book. The *superlative, est*; as, the great*est* house, the small*est* book.

Several adjectives express a comparison less than the positive, others increase or diminish the regular degrees; as, whit*ish* white, *very* white, *pure* white; whit*er, considerable* whiter, *much* whiter; whit*est*, the *very* whitest, *much* the whitest *beyond all comparison*, so that there can be none *whiter*, nor *so white*.

We make an aukward use of the words *great* and *good*, in the comparison of things; as, a *good deal*, or *great deal* whiter; a *good* many men, or a *great* many men. As we never hear of a *small* deal, or a *bad* deal whiter, nor of a *bad many*, nor *little many*, it would be well to avoid such phrases.

The words which are added to other adjectives, to increase or diminish the comparison, or assist in their definition, may properly be called *secondary adjectives*, for such is their character. They do not refer to the thing to be *defined* or *described*, but to the adjective which is affected, in some way, by them. They are easily distinguished from the rest by noticing this fact. Take for example: "A *very dark red* raw silk lady's dress handkerchief." The resolution of this sentence would stand thus:

A (   ) handkerchief.
A (   ) *red* (   ) handkerchief.
A () *dark* red (   ) handkerchief.
A *very* dark red (   ) handkerchief.
A very dark red () *silk* (   ) handkerchief.
A very dark red *raw* silk (   ) handkerchief.
A very dark red raw silk   ()   *dress* handkerchief.
A very dark red raw silk *lady's* dress handkerchief.

We might also observe that *hand* is an adjective, compounded by use with *kerchief*. It is derived from the french word *couvrir*, to cover, and *chef*, the head. It means a head dress, a cloth to cover, a neck cloth, a napkin. By habit we apply it to a single article, and speak of *neck* handkerchief.

The nice shade of meaning, and the appropriate use of adjectives, is more distinctly marked in distinguishing colors than in any thing else, for the simple reason, that there is nothing in nature so closely observed. For instance, take the word *green*, derived from *grain*, because it is grain color, or the color of the fair carpet of nature in spring and summer. But this hue changes from the *deep grass green*, to the light olive, and words are chosen to express the thousand varying tints produced by as many different objects. In the adaptation of language to the expression of ideas, we do not separate these shades of color from the things in which such colors are supposed to reside. Hence we talk of *grass, pea, olive, leek, verdigris, emerald, sea*, and *bottle* green; also, of *light, dark, medium; very* light, or dark grass, pea, olive, or *invisible* green.

Red, as a word, means *rayed*. It describes the appearance or substance produced when *rayed*, reddened, or radiated by the morning beams of the sun, or any other *radiating* cause.

Wh is used for *qu,* in white, which means *quite, quited, quitted, cleared, cleansed* of all *color, spot,* or *stain.*

Blue is another spelling for *blew.* Applied to color, it describes something in appearance to the sky, when the clouds and mists are *blown* away, and the clear *blue ether* appears.

You will be pleased with the following extract from an eloquent writer of the last century,[9] who, tho somewhat extravagant in some of his speculations, was, nevertheless, a close observer of nature, which he studied as it is, without the aid of human theories. The beauty of the style, and the correctness of the sentiment, will be a sufficient apology for its length.

"We shall employ a method, not quite so learned, to convey an idea of the generation of colors, and the decomposition of the solar ray. Instead of examining them in a prism of glass, we shall consider them in the heavens, and there we shall behold the five primordial colours *unfold themselves* in the order which we have indicated.

"In a fine summer's night, when the sky is loaded only with some light vapours, sufficient to stop and to refract the rays of the sun, walk out into an open plain, where the first fires of Aurora may be perceptible. You will first observe the horizon *whiten* at the spot where she is to make her appearance; and this radiance, from its colour, has procured for it, in the French language, the name of *aube,* (the dawn,) from the Latin word *alba,* white. This whiteness insensibly ascends in the heavens, *assuming* a tint of yellow some degrees above the horizon; the yellow as it rises passes into orange; and this shade of orange rises upward into the lively vermilion, which extends as far as the zenith. From that point you will perceive in the heavens behind you the violet succeeding the vermilion, then the azure, after it the deep blue or indigo colour, and, last of all, the black, quite to the westward.

"Though this display of colours presents a multitude of intermediate shades, which rapidly succeed each other, yet at the moment the sun is going to exhibit his disk, the dazzling white is visible in the horizon, the pure yellow at an elevation of forty-five degrees; the fire color in the zenith; the pure blue forty-five degrees under it, toward the west; and in the very west the dark veil of night still lingering on the horizon. I think I have remarked this progression between the tropics, where there is scarcely any horizontal refraction to make the light prematurely encroach on the darkness, as in our climates.

"Sometimes the trade-winds, from the north-east or south-east, blow there, card the clouds through each other, then sweep them to the west, crossing and recrossing them over one another, like the osiers interwoven in a transparent basket. They throw over the sides of this chequered work the clouds which are not employed in the contexture, roll them up into enormous masses, as white as snow, draw them out along their extremities in the form of a crupper, and pile them upon each other, moulding them into the shape of mountains, caverns, and rocks; afterwards, as evening approaches, they grow somewhat calm, as if afraid of deranging their own workmanship. When the sun sets behind this magnificent netting, a multitude of luminous rays are transmitted through the interstices, which produce such an effect, that the two sides of the lozenge illuminated by them have the appearance of being girt with gold, and the other two in the shade seem tinged with *ruddy* orange. Four or five divergent streams of light, emanated from the setting sun up to the zenith, *clothe* with fringes of gold the undeterminate summits of this celestial barrier, and strike with the reflexes of their fires the pyramids of the collateral aerial mountains, which then appear to consist of *silver* and *vermilion*. At this moment of the evening are perceptible, amidst their redoubled ridges, a multitude of valleys extending into infinity, and distinguishing themselves at their opening by some shade of flesh or of rose colour.

"These celestial valleys present in their different contours inimitable tints of white, melting away into white, or shades lengthening themselves out without mixing over other shades. You see, here and there, issuing from the cavernous sides of those mountains, tides of *light* precipitating themselves, in ingots of gold and silver, over rocks of coral. Here it is a gloomy rock, pierced through and through, disclosing, beyond the aperture, the pure azure of the firmament; there it is an extensive strand, covered with sands of gold, stretching over the rich ground of heaven; *poppy-coloured, scarlet,* and *green* as the emerald.

"The reverberation of those western colours diffuses itself over the sea, whose azure billows it *glazes* with saffron and purple. The mariners, leaning over the gunwale of the ship, admire in silence those aerial landscapes. Sometimes this sublime spectacle presents itself to them at the hour of prayer, and seems to invite them to lift up their hearts with their voices to the heavens. It changes every instant into forms as variable as the shades, presenting celestial colors and forms which no pencil can pretend to imitate, and no language can describe.

"Travellers who have, at various seasons, ascended to the summits of the highest mountains on the globe, never could perceive, in the clouds below them, any thing but a gray and lead-colored surface, similar to that of a lake. The sun, notwithstanding, illuminated them with his whole light; and his rays might there combine all the laws of refraction to which our systems of physics have subjected them. Hence not a single shade of color is employed in vain, through the universe; those celestial decorations being made for the level of the earth, their magnificent point of view taken from the habitation of man.

"These admirable concerts of lights and forms, manifest only in the lower region of the clouds the least illuminated by the sun, are produced by laws with which I am totally unacquainted. But the whole are reducible to five colors: yellow, a generation from white; red, a deeper shade of yellow; blue, a strong tint of red; and black, the extreme tint of blue. This progression cannot be doubted, on observing in the morning the expansion of the light in the heavens. You there see those five colors, with their intermediate shades, generating each other nearly in this order: white, sulphur yellow, lemon yellow, yolk of egg yellow, orange, aurora color, poppy red, full red, carmine red, purple, violet, azure, indigo, and black. Each color seems to be only a strong tint of that which precedes it, and a faint tint of that which follows; thus the whole together appear to be only modulations of a progression, of which white is the first term, and black the last.

"Indeed trade cannot be carried on to any advantage, with the Negroes, Tartars, Americans, and East-Indians, but through the medium of red cloths. The testimonies of travellers are unanimous respecting the preference universally given to this color. I have indicated the universality of this taste, merely to demonstrate the falsehood of the philosophic axiom, that tastes are arbitrary, or that there are in Nature no laws for beauty, and that our tastes are the effects of prejudice. The direct contrary of this is the truth;

prejudice corrupts our natural tastes, otherwise the same over the whole earth.

"With red Nature heightens the brilliant parts of the most beautiful flowers. She has given a complete clothing of it to the rose, the queen of the garden: and bestowed this tint on the blood, the principle of life in animals: she invests most of the feathered race, in India, with a plumage of this color, especially in the season of love; and there are few birds without some shades, at least, of this rich hue. Some preserve entirely the gray or brown ground of their plumage, but glazed over with red, as if they had been rolled in carmine; others are besprinkled with red, as if you had blown a scarlet powder over them.

"The red (or *rayed*) color, in the midst of the five primordial colors, is the harmonic expression of them by way of excellence; and the result of the union of two contraries, light and darkness. There are, besides, agreeable tints, compounded of the oppositions of extremes. For example, of the second and fourth color, that is, of yellow and blue, is formed green, which constitutes a very beautiful harmony, and ought, perhaps, to possess the second rank in beauty, among colors, as it possesses the second in their generation. Nay, green appears to many, if not the most beautiful tint, at least the most lovely, because it is less dazzling than red, and more congenial to the eye."

Many words come under the example previously given to illustrate the secondary character of adjectives, which should be carefully noticed by the learner, to distinguish whether they define or describe things, or are added to increase the distinction made by the adjectives themselves, for both defining and describing adjectives admit of this addition; as, *old* English coin, New England rebelion; a mounted whip, and a *gold* mounted sword—not a gold sword; a *very fine* Latin scholar.

Secondary adjectives, also, admit of comparison in various ways; as, *dearly* beloved, a *more* beloved, the *best* beloved, the *very* best beloved brother.

Words formerly called "prepositions," admit of comparison, as I have before observed. "Benhadad fled into an *inner* chamber." The in*ner* temple. The in*most* recesses of the heart. The *out* fit of a squadron. The out*er* coating of a vessel, or house. The ut*most* reach of grammar. The *up* and *down* hill side of a field. The up*per* end of the lot. The upper*most* seats. A part *of* the book. Take it *farther off.* The *off* cast. India *beyond* the Ganges. Far beyond the boundaries of the nation. I shall go *to* the city. I am *near to* the town. *Near* does not *qualify the verb*, for it has nothing to do with it. I can exist in one place as well as another. It is *below* the surface; *very far* below it. It is above the earth—"high above all height."

Such expressions frequently occur in the expression of ideas, and are correctly understood; as difficult as it may have been to describe them with the theories learned in the books—sometimes calling them one thing, sometimes another—when their character and meaning was unchanged, or, according to old systems, had "no meaning at all of their own!"

But I fear I have gone *far* beyond your patience, and, perhaps, entered *deeper* into this subject than was necessary, to enable you to discover my meaning. I desired to make the subject *as* distinct *as* possible, that all might see the important improvement suggested. I am apprehensive even now, that some will be compelled to *think* many *profound thoughts* before they will see the end of the obscurity under which they have long been shrouded, in reference to the false rules which they have been taught. But we have one consolation—those who are not bewildered by the grammars they have tried in vain to understand, will not be very likely to make a wrong use of adjectives, especially if they have ideas to express; for there is no more danger of mistaking an adjective for a noun, or verb, than there is of mistaking a *horse* chestnut for a *chestnut* horse.

In our next we shall commence the consideration of Verbs, the most important department in the science of language, and particularly so in the system we are defending. I hope you have not been uninterested thus far in the prosecution of the subject of language, and I am confident you will not be in what remains to be said upon it. The science, so long regarded *dry* and uninteresting, becomes delightful and easy; new and valuable truths burst upon us at each advancing step, and we feel to bless God for the ample means afforded us for obtaining knowledge from, and communicating it to others, on the most important affairs of time and eternity.

LECTURE VIII.

ON VERBS.

Unpleasant to expose error. — Verbs defined. — Every thing acts. — Actor and object. — Laws. — Man. — Animals. — Vegetables. — Minerals. — Neutrality degrading. — Nobody can explain a neuter verb. — *One* kind of verbs. — *You* must decide. — Importance of teaching children the truth. — Active verbs. — Transitive verbs false. — Samples. — Neuter verbs examined. — Sit. — Sleep. — Stand. — Lie. — Opinion of Mrs. W. — Anecdote.

We now come to the consideration of that class of words which in the formation of language are called *Verbs*. You will allow me to bespeak your favorable attention, and to insist most strenuously on the propriety of a free and thoro examination into the nature and use of these words. I shall be under the necessity of performing the thankless task of exposing the errors of honest, wise, and good men, in order to remove difficulties which have long existed in works on language, and clear the way for a more easy and consistent explanation of this interesting and essential department of literature. I regret the necessity for such labors; but no person who wishes the improvement of mankind, or is willing to aid the growth of the human intellect, in its high aspirations after truth, knowledge, and goodness, should shrink from a frank exposition of what he deems to be error, nor refuse his assistance, feeble tho it may be, in the establishment of correct principles.

In former lectures we have confined our remarks to things and a description of their characters and relations, so that every entity of which we can conceive a thought, or concerning which we can form an expression, has been defined and described in the use of nouns and adjectives. Every thing in creation, of which we think, material or immaterial, real or imaginary, and to which we give a name, to represent the idea of it, comes under the class of words called nouns. The words which specify or distinguish one thing from another, or describe its properties, character, or relations, are designated as adjectives. There is only one other employment left for words, and that is the expression of the actions, changes, or inherent tendencies of things. This important department of knowledge is, in grammar, classed under the head of VERBS.

Verb is derived from the Latin *verbum*, which signifies a *word*. By specific application it is applied to those *words* only which express action, correctly understood; the same as Bible, derived from the Greek "*biblos*" means literally *the book*, but, by way of eminence, is applied to the sacred scriptures only.

This interesting class of words does not deviate from the correct principles which we have hitherto observed in these lectures. It depends on established laws, exerted in the regulation of matter and thought; and whoever would learn its sublime use must be a close observer of things, and the mode of their existence. The important character it sustains in the production of ideas of the changes and tendencies of things and in the transmission of thought, will be found simple, and obvious to all.

Things exist; Nouns name them.

Things differ; Adjectives define or describe them.

Things act; Verbs express their actions.

    All Verbs denote action.

By action, we mean not only perceivable motion, but an inherent tendency to change, or resist action. It matters not whether we speak of animals possessed of the power of locomotion; of vegetables, which *send* forth their branches, leaves, blossoms, and fruits; or of minerals, which *retain* their forms, positions, and properties. The same principles are concerned, the same laws exist, and should be observed in all our attempts to understand their operations, or employ them in the promotion of human good. Every thing acts according to the ability it possesses; from the small particle of sand, which *occupies* its place upon the sea shore, up thro the various gradation of being, to the tall archangel, who *bows* and *worships* before the throne of the uncreated Cause of all things and actions which exist thro out his vast dominions.

As all actions presuppose an *actor*, so every action must result on some *object*. No effect can exist without an efficient cause to produce it; and no cause can exist without a corresponding effect resulting from it. These mutual relations, helps, and dependencies, are manifest in all creation. Philosophy, religion, the arts, and all science, serve only to develope these primary laws of nature, which unite and strengthen, combine and regulate, preserve and guide the whole. From the Eternal I AM, the uncreated, self-existent, self-sustaining CAUSE of all things, down to the minutest particle of dust, evidences may be traced of the existence and influence of these laws, in themselves irresistible, exceptionless, and immutable. Every thing has a place and a duty assigned it; and harmony, peace, and perfection are the results of a careful and judicious observance of the laws given for its regulation. Any infringement of these laws will produce disorder, confusion, and distraction.

Man is made a little lower than the angels, possessed of a mind capable of reason, improvement, and happiness; an intellectual soul inhabiting a mortal body, the connecting link between earth and heaven—the material and spiritual world. As a physical being, he is subject, in common with other things, to the laws which regulate matter: as an intellectual being, he is governed by the laws which regulate mind: as possessed of both a body and mind, a code of moral laws demand his observance in all the social relations and duties of life. Obedience to these laws is the certain source of health of body, and peace of mind. An infringement of them will as certainly be attended with disease and suffering to the one, and sorrow and anguish to the other.

Lower grades of animals partake of many qualities in common with man. In some they are deficient; in others they are superior. Some animals are possessed of all but reason, and even in that, the highest of them come very little short of the lowest of the human species. If they have not reason, they possess an instinct which nearly approaches it. These qualities dwindle down gradually thro the various orders and varieties of animated nature, to the lowest grade of animalculæ, a multitude of which may inhabit a single drop of water; or to the zoophytes and lythophytes, which form the connecting link between the animal and vegetable kingdom; as the star-fish, the polypus, and spunges. Then strike off into another kingdom, and observe the laws vegetable life. Mark the tall pine which has grown from a small seed which *sent* forth its root downwards and its trunk upwards, drawing nourishment from earth, air, and water, till it now waves its top to the passing breeze, a hundred feet above this dirty earth: or the oak or olive, which have *maintained* their respective positions a dozen centuries despite the operations of wind and weather, and have shed their foliage and their seeds to propagate their species and extend their kinds to different places. While a hundred generations have lived and died, and the country often changed masters, they resist oppression, scorn misrule, and retain rights and privileges which are slowly encroached upon by the inroads of time, which will one day triumph over them, and they fall helpless to the earth, to submit to the chemical operations which shall dissolve their very being and cause them to mingle with the common dust, yielding their strength to give life and power to other vegetables which shall occupy their places.[10] Or mark the living principle in the "sensitive plant," which withers at every touch, and suffers long ere it regains its former vigor.

Descend from thence, down thro the various gradations of vegetable life, till you pass the narrow border and enter the mineral world. Here you will see displayed the same sublime principle, tho in a modified degree. Minerals *assume* different shapes, hues and relations; they increase and diminish, attach and divide under various circumstances, all the while *retaining* their identity and properties, and exerting their abilities according to the means they possess, till compelled to yield to a superior power, and learn to submit to the laws which operate in every department of this mutable world.

Every thing *acts* according to the ability God has bestowed upon it; and man can do no more. He has authority over all things on earth, and yet he is made to depend upon all. His authority extends no farther than a privilege, under wholesome restrictions, of making the whole subservient to his real good. When he goes beyond this, he usurps a power which belongs not to him, and the destruction of his happiness pays the forfeit of his imprudence. The injured power rises triumphant over the aggressor, and the glory of God's government, in the righteous and immediate execution of his laws, is clearly revealed. So long as man obeys the laws which regulate health, observes temperance in all things, uses the things of this world as not abusing them, he is at rest, he is blessed, he is happy: but no sooner has he violated heaven's law than he becomes the slave, and the servant assumes the master. But I am digressing. I would gladly follow this subject further, but I shall go beyond my limits, and, it may be, your patience.

I would insist, however, on the facts to which your attention has been given, for it is impossible, as I have before contended, to use language correctly without a knowledge of the things and ideas it is employed to represent.

Grovelling, indeed, must be the mind which will not trace the sublime exhibitions of Divine power and skill in all the operations of nature; and false must be that theory which teaches the young mind to think and speak of neutrality as attached to things which do exist. As low and debasing as the speculations of the schoolmen were, they gave to things which they conceived to be incapable of action, a principle which they called "*vis inertiæ*," or, *power to lie still*. Shall our systems of instruction descend below them, throw an insurmountable barrier in the way of human improvement, and teach the false principles that actions can exist without an effect, or that there is a class of words which "express neither action or passion." Such a theory is at war with the first principles of philosophy, and denies that "like causes produce like effects."

The ablest minds have never been able to explain the foundation of a "neuter verb," or to find a single word, with a solitary exception, which does not, in certain conditions, express a positive action, and terminate on a definite object; and that exception we shall see refers to a verb which expresses the highest degree of conceivable action. Still they have insisted on *three* and some on *four* kinds of verbs, one expressing action, another passion or suffering, and the third neutrality. We propose to offer a brief review of these distinctions, which have so long perplexed, not only learners, but teachers themselves, and been the fruitful source of much dissention among grammarians.

It is to be hoped you will come up to this work with as great candor as you have heretofore manifested, and as fully resolved to take nothing for granted, because it has been said by good or great men, and to reject nothing because it appears new or singular. Let truth be our object and reason our guide to direct us to it. We can not fail of arriving at safe and correct conclusions.

Mr. Murray tells us that "verbs are of three kinds, *active*, *passive*, and *neuter*. In a note he admits of "active *transitive* and intransitive verbs," as a subdivision of his first kind. Most of his "improvers" have adopted this distinction, and regard it as of essential importance.

We shall contend, as before expressed, that *all* verbs are of *one kind*, that they *express action*, for the simple yet sublime reason, that every thing acts, at all times, and under every possible condition; according to the true definition of *action* as understood and employed by all writers on grammar, and natural and moral science. Here we are at issue. Both, contending for principles so opposite, can not be correct. One or the other, however pure the motives, must be attached to a system wrong in theory, and of course pernicious in practice. You are to be the umpires in the case, and, if you are faithful to your trust, you will not be bribed or influenced in the least by the opinions of others. If divested of all former attachments, if free from all prejudice, there can be no doubt of the safety and correctness of your conclusions. But I am apprehensive I expect too much, if I place the *new* system of grammar on a footing equally favorable in your minds with those you have been taught to respect, as the only true expositions of language, from your childhood up, and which are recommended to you on the authority of the learned and good of many generations. I have to combat early prejudices, and systems long considered as almost sacred. But I have in my favor the common sense of the world, and a feeling of opposition to existing systems, which has been produced, not so much by a detection of their errors, as by a lack of capacity, as the learner verily thought, to understand their profound mysteries. I am, therefore, willing to risk the final decision with you, if *you* will decide. But I am not willing to have you made the tools of the opposite party, determined, whether convinced or not, to hold to your old *neuter* verb systems, right or wrong, merely because others are doing so. All I ask is *your* adoption of what is proved to be undeniably true, and rejection of whatever is found to be false.

Here is where the matter must rest, for it will not be pretended that it is better to teach falsehood because it is ancient and popular, than truth because it is novel. Teachers, in this respect, stand in a most responsible relation to their pupils. They should always insist with an unyielding pertinacity, on the importance of truth, and the evils of error. Every trifling incident, in the course of education, which will serve to show the contrast, should be particularly observed. If an error can be detected in their books, they should be so taught as to be able to correct it; and they should be so inclined as to be willing to do it. They should not be skeptics, however, but close observers, original thinkers, and correct reasoners. It is degrading to the true dignity and independence of man, to submit blindly to any proposition. Freedom of thought is the province of all. Children should be made to breathe the free air of honest inquiry, and to inhale the sweet spirit of truth and charity. They should not study their books as the end of learning, but as a means of knowing. Books should be regarded as lamps, which are set by the way side, not as the objects to be looked at, but the aids by which we may find the object of our search. Knowledge and usefulness constitute the leading motives in all study, and no occasion should be lost, no means neglected, which will lead the young mind to their possession.

Your attention is now invited to some critical remarks on the distinctions usually observed in the use of verbs. Let us carefully examine the meaning of these *three kinds* and see if there is any occasion for such a division; if they have any foundation in truth, or application in the correct use of language. We will follow the arrangements adopted by the most popular grammars.

"A *verb active* expresses an action, and necessarily implies an agent, and an object acted upon; as, to love, I love Penelope." A very excellent definition, indeed! Had grammarians stopped here, their works would have been understood, and proved of some service in the study of language. But when they diverge from this bright spot in the consideration of verbs—this oasis in the midst of a desert—they soon become lost in the surrounding darkness of conjecture, and follow each their own dim light, to hit on a random track, which to follow in the pursuit of their object.

We give our most hearty assent to the above definition of a verb. It expresses action, which necessarily implies an *actor*, and an *object* influenced by the action. In our estimation it matters not whether the object on which the action terminates is expressed or *understood*. If I *love*, I must love some object; either my neighbor, my enemy, my family, *myself*, or something else. In either case the *action* is the same, tho the objects may be different; and it is regarded, on all hands, as an active verb. Hence when the object on which the action terminates is not expressed, it is necessarily understood. All language is, in this respect, more or less eliptical, which adds much to its richness and brevity.

Active verbs, we are told, are divided into *transitive* and *intransitive*. Mr. Murray does not exactly approve of this distinction, but prefers to class the intransitive and neuter together. Others, aware of the fallacy of attempting to make children conceive any thing like neutrality in the verbs, *run, fly, walk, live,* &c., have preferred to mark the distinction and call them *in*transitive; because, say they, they do not terminate on any object expressed.

A *transitive verb* "expresses an action which passes from the agent to the object; as, Cæsar conquered Pompey." To this definition we can not consent. It attempts a distinction where there is none. It is not true in principle, and can not be adopted in practice.

"Cæsar conquered Pompey." Did the act of conquering pass *transitively* over from *Cæsar* to Pompey? They might not have seen each other during the whole battle, nor been within many miles of each other. They, each of them, stood at the head of their armies, and alike gave orders to their subordinate officers, and they again to their inferiors, and so down, each man contending valiantly for *victory*, till, at last, the fate of the day sealed the downfall of Pompey, and placed the crown of triumph on the head of Cæsar. The expression is a correct one, but the action expressed by the verb "conquered," is not transitive, as that term is understood. A whole train of causes was put in operation which finally terminated in the defeat of one, and the conquest of the other.

"Bonaparte *lost* the battle of Waterloo." What did *he* do to *lose* the battle? He exerted his utmost skill to *gain* the battle and escape defeat. He did not do a single act, he entertained not a single thought, which lead to such a result; but strove against it with all his power. If the fault was *his*, it was because he failed to act, and not because he labored to *lose* the battle. He had too much at stake to adopt such a course, and no man but a teacher of grammar, would ever accuse him of *acting* to *lose* the battle.

"A man was sick; he desired to recover (his health). He took, for medicine, opium by mistake, and *lost* his life by it." Was he guilty of suicide? Certainly, if our grammars are true. But he *lost* his life in trying to get well.

"A man in America *possesses* property in Europe, and his children *inherit* it after his death." What do the children do to *inherit* this property, of which they know nothing?

"The geese, by their gabbling, *saved* Rome from destruction." How did the geese save the city? They made a noise, which waked the sentinels, who roused the soldiers to arms; they fought, slew many Gauls, and delivered the city.

"A man in New-York *transacts* business in Canton." How does he do it? He has an agent there to whom he sends his orders, and he transacts the business. But how does he get his letters? The clerk writes them, the postman carries them on board the ship, the captain commands the sailors, who work the ropes which unfurl the sails, the wind blows, the vessel is managed by the pilot, and after a weary voyage of several months, the letters are delivered to the agent, who does the business that is required of him.

The miser *denies* himself every comfort, and spends his whole life in hoarding up riches; and yet he dies and *leaves* his gold to be the possession of others.

Christians *suffer* insults almost every day from the Turks.

Windows *admit* light and *exclude* cold.

Who can discover any thing like *transitive* action—a passing from the agent to the object—in these cases? What transitive action do the windows perform to *admit the light*; or the christians, to *suffer insults*; or the miser, to *leave his money*? If there is neutrality any where, we would look for it here. The fact is, these words express *relative* action, as we shall explain when we come to the examination of the true character of the verb.

Neutrality signifies (transitive verb!) no action, and *neuter* verbs *express a state of being*! A class of words which can not act, which apply to things in a quiescent state, *perform* the transitive action of "*expressing* a state of being!"

Who does not perceive the inconsistency and folly of such distinctions? And who has not found himself perplexed, if not completely bewildered in the dark and intricate labyrinths into which he has been led by the false grammar books! Every attempt he has made to extricate himself, by the dim light of the "simplifiers," has only tended to bewilder him still more, till he is utterly confounded, or else abandons the study altogether.

An *intransitive* verb "denotes action which is confined to the actor, and does not pass over to another object; as, I sit, he lives, they sleep."

"A verb *neuter* expresses neither action nor passion, but being, or a state of being; as, I am, I sleep, I sit."

These verbs are nearly allied in character; but we will examine them separately and fairly. The examples are the same, with exception of the verb *to be*, which we will notice by itself, and somewhat at large, in another place.

Our first object will be to ascertain the *meaning* and use of the words which have been given as samples of neutrality. It is unfortunate for the neuter systems that they can not define a "neuter verb" without making it express an action which terminates on some object.

"The man *sits* in his chair."

Sits, we are told, is a neuter verb. What does it mean? The man *places* himself in a sitting posture in his *seat*. He *keeps* himself in his chair by muscular energy, assisted by gravitation. The chair *upholds* him in that condition. Bring a small child and *sit* it (active verb,) in a chair beside him. Can it *sit*? No; it falls upon the floor and is injured. Why did it fall? It was not able to *keep* itself from falling. The lady fainted and *fell* from her *seat*. If there is no action in sitting, why did she not remain as she was? A company of ladies and gentlemen from the boarding school and college, entered the parlor of a teacher of neuter verbs; and he asked them to *sit* down, or be *seated.* They were neutral. He called them impolite. But they replied, that *sit* "expresses neither action nor passion," and hence he could not expect them to occupy his seats.

"*Sit* or *set* it away; *sit* near me; *sit* farther along; *sit* still;" are expressions used by every teacher in addressing his scholars. On the system we are examining, what would they understand by such inactive expressions? Would he not correct them for disobeying his orders? But what did he order them to do? Nothing at all, if *sit* denotes no action.

"I *sat* me down and wept."

"He *sat him* down by a pillar's base,
And drew his hand athwart his face."

Byron.

"Then, having shown his wounds, he'd *sit him* down,
And, all the live long day, discourse of war."

Tragedy of Douglass.

"But wherefore *sits he* there?
Death on my state! *This act* convinces me
That this retiredness of the duke and her,
Is plain contempt."

King Lear.

"*Sitting*, the *act of resting* on a seat.
Session, the *act of sitting*."

Johnson's Dictionary.

"*I sleep.*"

Is sleep a neuter verb? So we are gravely told by our authors. Can grammarians follow their own rules? If so, they may spend the "live long night" and "its waking hours," without resorting to "tired nature's sweet restorer, balmy sleep;" for there is no process under heaven whereby they can procure sleep, unless they *sleep* it. For one, I can never *sleep* without sleeping *sleep*—sometimes only a short *nap*. It matters not whether the object is expressed or not. The action remains the same. The true object is necessarily understood, and it would be superfluous to name it. Cases, however, often occur where, both in speaking and writing, it becomes indispensable to mention the object. "The stout hearted have *slept* their sleep." "They shall *sleep* the *sleep* of death." "They shall *sleep* the perpetual *sleep*, and shall not awake." "*Sleep* on now and *take* your rest." The child was troublesome and the mother sung it to sleep, and it *slept itself* quiet. A lady took opium and *slept herself* to death. "Many persons sleep themselves into a kind of unnatural stupidity." Rip Van Winkle, according to the legend, *slept* away a large portion of a common life.

> "Sleep, sleep to-day, tormenting cares."

> "And *sleep* dull *cares* away."

Was your sleep refreshing last night? How did you procure it? Let a person who still adheres to his *neuter* verbs, that sleep expresses no action, and has no object on which it terminates, put his theory in practice; he may as well sleep with his eyes open, sitting up, as to *lie himself* upon his bed.

A man lodged in an open chamber, and while he was *sleeping* (doing nothing) he *caught* a severe *cold* (active transitive verb) and had a long *run* of the fever. Who does not see, not only the bad, but also the false philosophy of such attempted distinctions? How can you make a child discover any difference in the *act of sleeping*, whether there is an object after it, or not? Is it not the same? And is not the object necessarily implied, whether expressed or not? Can a person *sleep*, without procuring *sleep*?

"*I stand.*"

The man *stands* firm in his integrity. Another stands in a very precarious condition, and being unable to retain his hold, *falls* down the precipice and is killed. Who is killed? The man, surely. Why did he fall? Because he could not *stand*. But there is no *action* in *standing*, say the books.

"*Stand* by thyself, come not near me?" "*Stand* fast in the liberty wherewith Christ hath made you free, and *be* not again entangled in the yoke of bondage." "Let him that thinketh he *standeth*, take heed lest he *fall*." If it requires no act to *stand*, there can be no danger of falling.

"Two pillars stood together; the rest had fallen to the ground. The one on the right was quite perfect in all its parts. The other *resembled it* very much, except it had *lost* its capital, and *suffered* some other injuries." How could the latter column, while performing no action in *standing*, act *transitively*, according to our grammars, and do something to *resemble* the other? or, what did it do to *lose* its capital, and *suffer* other injury?

"To *lie*, or *lay*."

It has been admitted that the verbs before considered are often used as active verbs, and that there is, in truth, action expressed by them. But when the man has fallen from his seat and *lies* upon the floor, it is contended that he no longer acts, and that *lie* expresses no action. He has ceased from physical, muscular action regulated by his will, and is now subject to the common laws which govern matter.

Let us take a strong example. The book *lies* or *lays* on the desk. Now you ask, does that book perform any action in laying on the desk? I answer, yes; and I will prove it on the principles of the soundest philosophy, to the satisfaction of every one present. Nor will I deviate from existing grammars to do it, so far as real action is concerned.

The book *lies* on the desk. The desk *supports* the book. Will you parse *supports*? It is, according to every system, an active transitive verb. It has an objective case after it on which the action terminates. But what does the desk do to *support* the book? It barely resists the action which the book *performs* in lying on it. The action of the desk and book is reciprocal. But if the book does not act, neither can the desk act, for that only repels the force of the book in pressing upon it in its tendency towards the earth, in obedience to the law of gravitation. And yet our authors have told us that the desk is *active* in resisting no action of the book! No wonder people are unable to understand grammar. It violates the first principles of natural science, and frames to itself a code of laws, unequal, false, and exceptionable, which bear no affinity to the rest of the world, and will not apply in the expression of ideas.

I was once lecturing on this subject in one of the cities of New-York. Mrs. W., the distinguished teacher of one of the most popular Female Seminaries in our country, attended. At the close of one lecture she remarked that the greatest fault she had discovered in the new system, was the want of a class of words to express neutrality. Children, she said, conceived ideas of things in a quiescent state, and words should be taught them by which to communicate such ideas. I asked her for an example. She gave the rock in the side of the mountain. It had never moved. It could never act. There it had been from the foundation of the earth, and there it would remain unaltered and unchanged till time should be no longer. I remarked, that I would take another small stone and *lay* it on the great one which could never act, and now we say the great rock *upholds, sustains* or *supports* the small one—all active transitive verbs with an object expressed.

She replied, she would give it up, for it had satisfied her of a new principle which must be observed in the exposition of all language, which accords with *facts as developed in physical and mental science.*

I continued, not only does that rock act in resisting the force of the small one which lays upon it, but, by the attraction of gravitation it is able to *maintain* its *position* in the side of the mountain; by cohesion it *retains* its distinct identity and solidity, and repels all foreign bodies. It is also subject to the laws which govern the earth in its diurnal and annual revolutions, and moves in common with other matter at the astonishing rate of a thousand miles in an hour! Who shall teach children, in these days of light and improvement, the grovelling doctrine of neutrality, this relic of the peripatetic philosophy? Will parents send their children to school to learn falsehood? And can teachers be satisfied to remain in ignorance, following with blind reverence the books they have studied, and refuse to examine new principles, fearing they shall be compelled to acknowledge former errors and study new principles? They should remember it is wiser and more honorable to confess a fault and correct it, than it is to remain permanent in error.

Let us take another example of the verb "*to lie.*" A country pedagogue who has followed his authorities most devotedly, and taught his pupils that *lie* is a "*neuter verb,* expressing neither action nor passion, but simply being, or a state of being," goes out, during the intermission, into a grove near by, to *exercise himself.* In attempting to roll a log up the hill, he *makes* a mis-step, and *falls* (intransitive verb, *nothing* falls!) to the ground, and the log *rolls* (*nothing*) on to him, and *lies* across his legs. In this condition he is observed by his scholars to whom he cries (nothing) for help. "Do (nothing) come (intransitive) and help me." They obey him and remain *neuter,* or at least act *intransitively,* and produce no effects. He cries again for help and his *cries* are regarded. They *present* themselves before him. "Do roll this log off; it will break my legs." "Oh no, master; how can that be? The log *lies* on you, does it not?" "Yes, and it will *press me* to death." "No, no; that can never be. The log can not act. Lies is a *neuter* verb, signifying neither *action* nor passion, but simply being or a state of being. You have a *state* of being, and the log has a state of being. It can not harm you. You must have forgotten the practical application of the truths you have been teaching us." It would be difficult to explain neuter verbs in such a predicament.

"Now I *lay* me down *to sleep*."

"She died and they *laid her* beside her lover under the spreading branches of the willow."

"They *laid it* away so secure that they could never find it."

They *laid* down to *rest themselves* after the fatigue of a whole day's journey.

We have now considered the model verbs of the neuter kind, with the exception of the verb TO BE, which is left for a distinct consideration, being the most active of all verbs. It is unnecessary to spend much time on this point. The errors I have examined have all been discovered by teachers of language, long ago, but few have ventured to correct them. An alleviation of the difficulty has been sought in the adoption of the intransitive verb, which "expresses an action that is confined to the actor or agent."

The remarks which have been given in the present lecture will serve as a hint to the course we shall adopt in treating of them, but the more particular examination of their character and uses, together with some general observation on the agents and objects of verbs, will be deferred to our next lecture.

LECTURE IX.

ON VERBS.

Neuter and intransitive. — Agents. — Objects. — No actions as such can be known distinct from the agent. — Imaginary actions. — Actions known by their effects. — Examples. — Signs should guide to things signified. — Principles of action. — POWER. — Animals. — Vegetables. — Minerals. — All things act. — Magnetic needle. — CAUSE. — Explained. — First Cause. — MEANS. — Illustrated. — Sir I. Newton's example. — These principles must be known. — RELATIVE action. — Anecdote of Gallileo.

We resume the consideration of verbs. We closed our last lecture with the examination of *neuter verbs*, as they have been called. It appears to us that evidence strong enough to convince the most skeptical was adduced to prove that *sit, sleep, stand* and *lie*, stand in the same relation to language as other verbs, that they do not, in any case, express neutrality, but frequently admit an objective word after them. These are regarded as the most neutral of all the verbs except *to be*, which, by the way, expresses the highest degree of action, as we shall see when we come to inquire into its meaning.

Grammarians have long ago discovered the falsity of the books in the use of a large portion of verbs which have been called neuter. To obviate the difficulty, some of them have adopted the distinction of *Intransitive* verbs, which express action, but terminate on no object; others still use the term *neuter*, but teach their scholars that when the *object* is *expressed*, it is active. This distinction has only tended to perplex learners, while it afforded only a temporary expedient to teachers, by which to dodge the question at issue. So far as the action is concerned, which it is the business of the verb to express, what is the difference whether "I *run*, or *run* myself?" "A man started in haste. He *ran* so fast that he *ran himself* to death." I strike

Thomas, Thomas *strikes David*, Thomas *strikes himself*. Where is the difference in the action? What matters it whether the action passes over to another object, or is confined within itself?

"But," says the objector, "you mistake. An intransitive verb is one where the 'effect is confined within the subject, and does not pass over to any object.'"

Very well, I think I understand the objection. When Thomas strikes David the effects of the blow *passes over* to him. And when he strikes himself, it "is confined within the subject," and hence the latter is an *intransitive* verb.

"No, no; there is an object on which the action terminates, in that case, and so we must call it a *transitive* verb."

Will you give me an example of an *intransitive* verb?

"I *run*, he *walks*, birds *fly*, it *rains*, the fire *burns*. No objects are expressed after these words, so the action is confined within themselves."

I now get your meaning. When the object is *expressed* the verb is transitive, when it is not it is intransitive. This distinction is generally observed in teaching, however widely it may differ from the intention of the makers of grammars. And hence children acquire the habit of limiting their inquiries to what they see placed before them by others, and do not think for themselves. When the verb has an objective word after it *expressed*, they are taught to attach action to it; but tho the action may be even greater, if the object is not expressed, they consider the action as widely different in its character, and adopt the false philosophy that a cause can exist without an effect resulting from it.

We assume this ground, and we shall labor to maintain it, that every verb necessarily presupposes an *agent* or *actor*, an *action*, and an *object* acted upon, or affected by the action.

No action, as such, can be known to exist separate from the thing that acts. We can conceive no idea of action, only by keeping our minds fixed on the acting substance, marking its changes, movements, and tendencies. "The book *moves*." In this case the eye rests on the book, and observes its positions and attitudes, alternating one way and the other. You can separate no action from the book, nor conceive any idea of it, as a separate entity.

Let the book be taken away. Where now is the action? What can you think or say of it? There is the same space just now occupied by the book, but no action is perceivable.

The boy *rolls* his marble upon the floor. All his ideas of the action performed by it are derived from an observation of the marble. His eye follows it as it moves along the floor. He sees it in that acting condition. When he speaks of the action as a whole, he thinks where it started and where it stopped. It is of no importance, so far as the verb is concerned, whether the marble received an impulse from his hand, or whether the floor was sufficiently inclined to allow it to roll by its own inherent tendency. The action is, in this case, the obvious change of the marble.

Our whole knowledge of action depends on an observance of things in a state of motion, or change, or exerting a tendency to change, or to counteract an opposing substance.

This will be admitted so far as material things are concerned. The same principle holds good in reference to every thing of which we form ideas, or concerning which we use language. In our definition of nouns we spoke of immaterial and imaginary things to which we gave *names* and which we consider as agencies capable of exerting an influence in the production of effects, or in resisting actions. It is therefore unimportant whether the action be real or imaginary. It is still inseparably connected with the thing that acts; and we employ it thus in the construction of language to express our thoughts. Thus, lions roar; birds sing; minds reflect; fairies dance; knowledge increases; fancies err; imagination wanders.

This fact should be borne in mind in all our attempts to understand or explain language. The mind should remain fixed to the acting substance, to observe its changes and relations at different periods, and in different circumstances. There is no other process by which any knowledge can be gained of actions. The mind contemplates the acting thing in a condition of change and determines the precise action by the *altered condition* of the thing, and thus learns to judge of actions by their effects. The only method by which we can know whether a *vegetable grows* or not is by comparing its form to-day with what it was some days ago. We can not decide on the improvement of our children only by observing the same rule.

"By their fruits ye shall know them," will apply in physics as well as in morals; for we judge of causes only by their effects. First principles can never be known. We observe things as they *are*, and remember how they *have been*; and from hence deduce our conclusions in reference to the *cause* of things we do not fully understand, or those consequences which will follow a condition of things as now existing. It is the business of philosophy to mark these effects, and trace them back to the causes which produced them, by observing all the intermediate changes, forms, attitudes, and conditions, in which such things have, at different times, been placed.

We say, "*trees grow*." But suppose no change had ever been observed in trees, that they had always been as they now are; in stature as lofty, in foliage as green and beautiful, in location unaltered. Who would then say, "trees grow?"

In this single expression a whole train of facts are taken into the account, tho not particularly marked. As a single expression we imply that *trees increase their stature*. But this we all know could never be effected without the influence of other causes. The soil where it stands must contain properties suited to the *growth* of the tree. A due portion of moisture and heat are also requisite. These facts all exist, and are indispensable to make good the expression that the "tree grows." We might also trace the capabilities of the tree itself, its roots, bark, veins or pores, fibres or grains, its succulent and absorbent powers. But, as in the case of the "man that killed the deer," noticed in a former lecture, the mind here conceives a single idea of a complete whole, which is signified by the single expression, "trees grow."

Let the following example serve in further illustration of this point. Take two bricks, the one heated to a high temperature, the other cold. Put them together, and in a short time you will find them of equal temperature. One has grown warm, the other cool. One has *imparted* heat and *received* cold, the other has *received* heat and *imparted* cold. Yet all this would remain forever unknown, but for the effects which must appear obvious to all. From these effects the causes are to be learned.

It must, I think, appear plain to all who are willing to see, that action, as such, can never exist distinct from the thing that acts; that all our notions of action are derived from an observance of *things* in an acting condition; and hence that no words can be framed to express our ideas of action on any other principle.

I hope you will bear these principles in mind. They are vastly important in the construction of language, as will appear when we come to speak of the *agents* and *objects* of action. We still adhere to the fact, that no rules of language can be successfully employed, which deviate from the permanent laws which operate in the regulation of matter and mind; a fact which can not be too deeply impressed on your minds.

In the consideration of actions as expressed by verbs, we must observe that *power, cause, means, agency,* and *effects,* are indispensable to their existence. Such principles exist *in fact,* and must be observed in obtaining a complete knowledge of language; for words, we have already seen, are the expression of ideas, and ideas are the impression of things.

In our attempts at improvement, we should strip away the covering, and come at the reality. Words should be measurably forgotten, while we search diligently for the things expressed by them. *Signs* should always conduct to the things *signified.* The weary traveller, hungry and faint, would hardly satisfy himself with an examination of the *sign* before the inn, marking its form, the picture upon it, the nice shades of coloring in the painting. He would go in, and search for the thing signified.

It has been the fault in teaching language, that learners have been limited to the mere *forms* of words, while the important duty of teaching them to look at the thing signified, has been entirely disregarded. Hence they have only obtained book knowledge. They know what the grammars say; but how to *apply* what they say, or what is in reality meant by it, they have yet to learn. This explains the reason why almost every man who has studied grammar will tell you that "he *used* to understand it, but it has all gone from him, for he has not looked into a *book* these many years." Has he lost a knowledge of language? Oh, no, he learned that before he saw a grammar, and will preserve it to the day of his death. What good did his two or three years study of grammar do him? None at all; he has forgotten all that he ever knew of it, and that is not much, for he only learned what some author said, and a few arbitrary rules and technical expressions which he could never understand nor apply in practice, except in special cases. But I wander. I throw in this remark to show you the necessity of bringing your minds to a close observance of things as they do in truth exist; and from them you can draw the principles of speech, and be able to use language correctly. For we still insist on our former opinion, that all language depends on the permanent laws of nature, as exerted in the regulation of matter and mind.

To return. I have said that all action denotes *power, cause, means, agency,* and *effects.*

Power depends on *physical energy,* or *mental skill.* I have hinted at this fact before. Things act according to the power or energy they possess. Animals walk, birds fly, fishes swim, minerals sink, poisons kill. Or, according to the adopted theories of naturalists:

Minerals *grow.*

Vegetables *grow* and *live.*

Animals *grow,* and *live,* and *feel.*

Every thing acts according to the ability it possesses. Man, possessed of reason, devises means and produces ends. Beasts change locations, devour vegetables, and sometimes other beasts. The lowest grade of animals never change location, but yet eat and live. Vegetables live and grow, but do not change location. They have the power to reproduce their species, and some of them to kill off surrounding objects. "The *carraguata* of the West Indies, clings round," says Goldsmith, "whatever tree it happens to approach; there it quickly gains the ascendant, and, loading the tree with a verdure not its own, keeps away that nourishment designed to feed the trunk, and at last entirely destroys its supporter." In our country, many gardens and fields present convincing proof of the ability of weeds to kill out the vegetables designed to grow therein. You all have heard of the *Upas,* which has a power sufficient to destroy the lives of animals and vegetables for a large distance around. Its very exhalations are death to whatever approaches it. It serves in metaphor to illustrate the noxious effects of all vice, of slander and deceit, the effects of which are to the moral constitution, what the tree itself is to natural objects, blight and mildew upon whatever comes within its reach.

Minerals are possessed of *power* no less astonishing, which may be observed whenever an opportunity is offered to call it forth. Active poisons, able to slay the most powerful men and beasts, lie hid within their bosoms. They have strong attractive and repelling powers. From the iron is made the strong cable which *holds* the vessel fast in her moorings, *enabling* it to outride the collected force of the winds and waves which *threaten* its destruction. From it also are manufactured the manacles which bind the strong man, or fasten the lion in his cage. Gold *possesses* a power which *charms* nearly all men to sacrifice their ease, and too many their moral principles, to pay their blind devotions at its shrine.

Who will contend that the power of action is confined to the animal creation alone, and that inanimate matter can not act? That there is a superior power possessed by man, endowed with an immaterial spirit in a corporeal body, none will deny. By the agency of the mind he can accomplish wonders, which mere physical power without the aid of such mental skill, could never perform. But with all his boasted superiority, he is often made the slave of inanimate things. His lofty powers of body and soul bend beneath the weight of accumulated sorrows, produced by the secret *operations* of contagious disease, which *slays* his wife, children, and friends, who fall like the ripened harvest before the gatherers scythe. Nay, he often submits to the controlling power of the vine, alcohol, or tobacco, which *gain* a secret influence over his nobler powers, and *fix* on him the stamp of disgrace, and *throw* around him fetters from which he finds it no easy matter to extricate himself. By the illusions of error and vice he is often betrayed, and long endures darkness and suffering, till he *regains* his native energies, and finds deliverance in the enjoyment of truth and virtue.

What is that secret power which lies concealed beyond the reach of human ken, and is transported from land to land unknown, till exposed in conditions suited to its operation, will show its active and resistless force in the destruction of life, and the devastation of whole cities or nations? You may call it plague, or cholera, or small pox, miasma, contagion, particles of matter floating in the air surcharged with disease, or any thing else. It matters not what you call it. It is sufficient to our present purpose to know that it has the ability to put forth a prodigious power in the production of consequences, which the highest skill of man is yet unable to prevent.

I might pursue this point to an indefinite length, and trace the secret powers possessed by all created things, as exhibited in the influence they exert in various ways, both as regards themselves and surrounding objects. But you will at once perceive my object, and the truth of the positions I assume. A common power pervades all creation, operating by pure and perfect laws, regulated by the Great First Cause, the Moving Principle, which guides, governs, and controls the whole.[11]

Degrading indeed must be those sentiments which limit all action to the animal frame as an organized body, moved by a living principle. Ours is a sublimer duty; to trace the operations of the Divine Wisdom which acts thro out all creation, in the minutest particle of dust which *keeps* its *position* secure, till moved by some superior power; or in the *needle* which points with unerring skill to its fixed point, and *guides* the vessel, freighted with a hundred lives, safe thro the midnight storm, to its destined haven; tho rocked by the waves and driven by the winds, it remains uninfluenced, and tremblingly alive to the important duties entrusted to its charge, continues its faithful service, and is watched with the most implicit confidence by all on board, as the only guide to safety. The same Wisdom is displayed thro out all creation; in the beauty, order, and harmony of the universe; in the planets which float in the azure vault of heaven; in the glow worm that glitters in the dust; in the fish which cuts the liquid element; in the pearl which sparkles in the bottom of the ocean; in every thing that lives, moves, or has a being; but more distinctly in man, created in the moral image of his Maker, possessed of a heart to feel, and a mind to understand—the third in the rank of intelligent beings.

I cannot refuse to favor you with a quotation from that inimitable poem, Pope's Essay on Man. It is rife with sentiment of the purest and most exalted character. It is direct to our purpose. You may have heard it a thousand times; but I am confident you will be pleased to hear it again.

> Ask for what end the heavenly bodies shine,
> Earth for whose use? Pride answers, "'Tis for mine:
> "For me kind nature wakes her genial pow'r,

"Suckles each herb, and spreads out every flow'r;
"Annual for me, the grape, the rose renew
"The juice nectareous, and the balmy dew;
"For me, the mine a thousand treasures brings;
"For me health gushes from a thousand springs;
"Seas roll to waft me, suns to light me rise;
"My footstool earth, my canopy the skies."

    But errs not nature from this gracious end,
From burning suns when livid deaths descend,
When earthquakes swallow, or when tempests sweep
Towns to one grave, whole nations to the deep?
"*No*," ('tis replied,) "*the first Almighty Cause
Acts not by partial, but by general laws;
Th' exceptions few; some change since all began:
And what created perfect?*" Why then man?
If the great end be human happiness,
Then nature deviates—and can man do less?
As much that end a constant course requires
Of show'rs and sunshine, as of man's desires;
As much eternal springs and cloudless skies,
As man forever temp'rate, calm, and wise.
If plagues or earthquakes break not heaven's design.
Why then a Borgia, or a Cataline?
Who knows but He whose hand the lightning forms,
Who heaves old ocean, and who wings the storms;
Pours fierce ambition in a Cæsar's mind;
Or turns young Ammon loose to scourge mankind?
From pride, from pride our very reas'ning springs;
Account for moral as for nat'ral things:
Why charge we heaven in those, in these acquit?
In both, to reason right, is to submit.

    Better for us, perhaps, it might appear,
Were there all harmony, all virtue here;
That never air or ocean felt the wind;
That never passion discomposed the mind.

But ALL subsists by elemental strife;
And passions are the elements of life.
The general ORDER, since the whole began,
Is kept in nature, and is kept in man.

    Look round our world, behold the chain of love.
Combining all below and all above;
See plastic nature working to this end,
The single atoms each to other tend;
Attract, attracted to, the next in place
Formed and impelled its neighbor to embrace,
See matter next, with various life endued,
Press to one center still the gen'ral good.
See dying vegetables life sustain,
See life dissolving, vegetate again;
All forms that perish, other forms supply,
(By turns we catch the vital breath, and die)
Like bubbles on the sea of matter borne,
They rise, they break, and to that sea return,
Nothing is foreign—parts relate to whole;
One all-extending, all-preserving soul
Connects each being greatest with the least;
Made beast in aid of man, and man of beast;
All served, all serving; nothing stands alone;
The chain holds on, and where it ends, unknown.

But *power* alone is not sufficient to produce action. There must be a CAUSE to call it forth, to set in operation and exhibit its latent energies. It will remain hid in its secret chambers till efficient causes have set in operation the *means* by which its existence is to be discovered in the production of change, effects, or results. There is, it is said, in every created thing a power sufficient to produce its own destruction, as well as to preserve its being. In the human body, for instance, there is a constant tendency to decay, to waste; which a counteracting power resists, and, with proper assistance, keeps alive.

The same may be said of vegetables which are constantly throwing off, or exhaling the waste, offensive, or useless matter, and yet a restoring power, assisted by heat, moisture, and the nourishment of the earth, resists the tendency to decay and preserves it alive and growing. The air, the earth, nay, the ocean itself, philosophers assure us, contain powers sufficient to self-destruction. But I will not enlarge here. Let the necessary *cause* be exerted which will give vent to this hidden power and actions the most astonishing and destructive would be the effect. These are often witnessed in the tremendous earthquakes which devastate whole cities, states, and empires; in the tornados which pass, like the genius of evil, over the land, levelling whatever is found in its course; or in the waterspouts and maelstroms which prove the grave of all that comes within their grasp.

In the attempted destruction of the royal family and parliament of England, by what is usually called the "gunpowder plot," the arrangements were all made; two hogsheads and thirty-six barrels of powder, sufficient to blow up the house of lords and the surrounding buildings, were secreted in a vault beneath it, strown over with faggots. Guy Fawkes, a spanish officer, employed for the purpose, lay at the door, on the 5th of November, 1605, with the matches, or *means*, in his pocket, which should set in operation the prodigious dormant *power*, which would hurl to destruction James I., the royal family, and the protestant parliament, give the ascendancy to the Catholics, and change the whole political condition of the nation. The *project* was discovered, the *means* were removed, the *cause* taken away, and the threatened *effects* were prevented.

The CAUSE of action is the immediate subject which precedes or tends to produce the action, without which it would not take place. It may result from volition, inherent tendency, or communicated impulse; and is known to exist from the effects produced by it, in the altered or new condition of the thing on which it operates; which change would not have been effected without it.

Causes are to be sought for by tracing back thro the effects which are produced by them. The factory is put in operation, and the cloth is manufactured. The careless observer would enter the building and see the spindles, looms, and wheels operated by the hands, and go away satisfied that he has seen enough, seen all. But the more careful will look farther. He will trace each band and wheel, each cog and shaft, down by the balance power, to the water race and floom; or thro the complicated machinery of the steam engine to the piston, condenser, water, wood, and fire; marking a new, more secret, and yet more efficient cause at each advancing step. But all this curiously wrought machinery is not the product of chance, operated without care. A superior cause must be sought in human skill, in the deep and active ingenuity of man. Every contrivance presupposes a contriver. Hence there must have been a power and means sufficient to combine and regulate the power of the water, or generate and direct the steam. That power is vested in man; and hence, man stands as the cause, in relation to the whole process operated by wheels, bands, spindles, and looms. Yet we may say, with propriety, that the water, or the steam; the water-wheel, or the piston; the shafts, bands, cogs, pullies, spindles, springs, treddles, harnesses, reeds, shuttles, an almost endless concatenation of instruments, are alike the *causes*, which tend to produce the final result; for let one of these intermediate causes be removed, and the whole power will be diverted, and all will go wrong—the effect will not be produced.

There must be a FIRST CAUSE to set in operation all inferior ones in the production of action; and to that *first* cause all action, nay, the existence of all other causes, may be traced, directly, or more distant. The intervening causes, in the consecutive order of things, may be as diversified as the links in the chain of variant beings. Yet all these causes are moved by the all-sufficient and ever present agency of the Almighty Father, the UNCAUSED CAUSE of all things and beings; who spoke into existence the universe with all its various and complicated parts and orders; who set the sun, moon, and stars in the firmament, gave the earth a place, and fixed the sea a bed; throwing around them barriers over which they can never pass. From the height of his eternal throne, his eye pervades all his works; from the tall archangel, that "adores and burns," down to the very hairs of our heads, which are all numbered, his wise, benevolent, and powerful supervision may be traced in legible lines, which may be seen and read of all men. And from effects, the most diminutive in character, may be traced back, from cause to cause, upward in the ascending scale of being, to the same unrivalled Source of all power, splendor, and perfection, the presence of Him, who spake, and it was done; who commanded, and it *stood still*; or, as the poet has it:

"Look thro nature up to nature's God."

The *means* of action are those aids which are displayed as the medium thro which existing causes are to exhibit their hidden powers in producing changes or effects. The matches in the pocket of Guy Fawkes were the direct means by which he intended to set in operation a train of causes which should terminate in the destruction of the house of lords and all its inmates. Those matches, set on fire, would convey a spark to the faggots, and thence to the powder, and means after means, and cause after cause, in the rapid succession of events, would ensue, tending to a final, inevitable, and melancholy result.

A ball shot from a cannon, receives its first impulse from the powder; but it is borne thro the air by the aid of a principle inherent in itself, which power is finally overcome by the density of the atmosphere which impedes its progress, and the law of gravitation finally attracts it to the earth. These contending principles may be known by observing the curved line in which the ball moves from the cannon's mouth to the spot where it rests. But if there is no power in the ball, why does not the ball of cork discharged from the same gun with the same momentum, travel to the same distance, at the same rate? The action commences in both cases with the same projectile force, the same exterior *means* are employed, but the results are widely different. The cause of this difference must be sought for in the comparative power of each substance to *continue its own movements*.

Every boy who has played at ball has observed these principles. He throws his ball, which, if not *counteracted*, will continue in a straight line, *ad infinitum*—without end. But the air impedes its progress, and gravitation brings it to the ground. When he throws it against a hard substance, its velocity is not only overcome, but it is sent back with great force. But if he takes a ball of wax, of snow, or any strong adhesive substance, it will not bound. How shall we account to him for this difference? He did the same with both balls. The impetus given the one was as great as the other, and the resistance of the intervening substance was as great in one case as the other; and yet, one bounds and rebounds, while the other sticks fast as a friend, to the first object it meets. The cause of this difference is to be sought for in the different capabilities of the respective balls. One possesses a strong elastic and repelling power; in the other, the attraction of cohesion is predominant.

Take another example. Let two substances of equal size and form, the one made of lead, the other of cork, be put upon the surface of a cistern of water. The external circumstances are the same, but the effects are widely different—one sinks, the other floats. We must look for the cause of this difference, not in the opposite qualities of surrounding matter, but in the things themselves. If you add to the cork another quality possessed by the lead, and give it the same form, size, and *weight*, it will as readily sink to the bottom. But this last property is possessed in different degrees by the two bodies, and hence, while the one floats upon the water, the other displaces its particles and sinks to the bottom. You may take another substance; say the mountain ebony, which is heavier than water, but lighter than lead, and immerse it in the water; it will not sink with the rapidity of lead, because its inherent *power* is not so strong.

Take still another case. Let two balls, suspended on strings, be equally, or, to use the technical term, *positively* electrified. Bring them within a certain distance, and they will repel each other. Let the electric fluid be extracted from one, and the other will attract it. Before, they were as enemies; now they embrace as friends. The magnet furnishes the most striking proof in favor of the theory we are laboring to establish. Let one of sufficient power be let down within the proper distance, it will overcome the power of gravitation, and *attract* the heavy steel to itself. What is the cause of this wonderful fact? Who can account for it? Who can trace out the hidden cause; the "*primum mobile*" of the Ptolmaic philosophy—the secret spring of motion? But who will dare deny that such effects do exist, and that they are produced by an efficient cause? Or who will descend into the still more dark and perplexing mazes of neuter verb grammars, and deny that matter has such a power to act?

These instances will suffice to show you what we mean when we say, *every thing acts according to the ability God has given it to act*. I might go into a more minute examination of the properties of matter, affinity, hardness, weight, size, color, form, mobility, &c., which even old grammars will allow it to *possess*; but I shall leave that work for you to perform at your leisure.

Whoever has any doubts remaining in reference to the abilities of all things to *produce, continue,* or *prevent* motion, will do well to consult the prince of philosophers, Sir Isaac Newton, who, after Gallileo, has treated largely upon the laws of motion. He asserts as a fact, full in illustration of the principles I am laboring to establish, that in ascending a hill, the trace rope pulls the horse back as much as he draws that forward, only the horse overcomes the resistance of the load, and moves it up the hill. On the old systems, no power would be requisite to move the load, for it could oppose no resistance to the horse; and the small child could move it with as much ease as the strong team.

Who has not an acquaintance sufficiently extensive to know these things? I can not believe there is a person present, who does not fully comprehend my meaning, and discover the correctness of the ground I have assumed. And it should be borne in mind, that no collection or arrangement of words can be composed into a sentence, which do not obtain their meaning from a connection of things as they exist and operate in the material and intellectual world, and that it is not in the power of man to frame a sentence, to think or speak, but in conformity with these general and exceptionless laws.

This important consideration meets us at every advancing step, as if to admonish us to abandon the vain project of seeking a knowledge of language without an acquaintance with the great principles on which it depends. To look for the leading rules of speech in set forms of expression, or in the capricious customs of any nation, however learned, is as futile as to attempt to gain a knowledge of the world by shutting ourselves up in a room, and looking at paintings and drawings which may be furnished by those who know as little of it as we do. How fallacious would be the attempt, how much worse than time thrown away, for the parent to shut up his child in a lonely room, and undertake to impress upon its mind a knowledge of man, beasts, birds, fish, insects, rivers, mountains, fields, flowers, houses, cities, &c., with no other aid than a few miserable pictures, unlike the reality, and in many respects contradictory to each other. And yet that would be adopting a course very similar to the one long employed as the only means of acquiring a knowledge of language; limited to a set of arbitrary, false, and contradictory rules, which the brightest geniuses could never understand, nor the most erudite employ in the expression of ideas.

The grammars, it was thought, must be studied to acquire the use of language, and yet they were forgotten before such knowledge was put in practice.

A simple remark on the principles of *relative* action, and we will pass to the consideration of *agents* and *objects*, or the more immediate *causes* and *effects* of action.

We go forth at the evening hour and look upon the sun *sinking* beneath the horizon; we mark the varying hues of light as they appear, and change, and fade away. We see the shades of night *approaching*, with a gradual pace, till the beautiful landscape on which we had been gazing, the hills and the meadows; the farm house and the cultivated fields, the grove, the orchard, and the garden; the tranquil lake and the babbling brook; the dairy returning home, and the lambkins gambolling beside their dams; all *recede* from our view, and *appear* to us no longer. All this is *relative* action. But so far as language and ideas are concerned, it matters not whether the sun actually *sinks* behind the hills, or the hills interpose between it and us; whether the landscape *recedes* from our view, or the shades of night intercept so as to obscure our vision. The habit of thought is the same, and the form of expression must agree with it. We say the sun *rises* and *sets*, in reference to the obvious fact, without stopping to inquire whether it really moves or not. Nor is such an inquiry at all necessary, as to matter of fact, for all we mean by such expressions, is, that by some process, immaterial to the case in hand, the sun stands in a new relation to the earth, its altitude is elevated or depressed, and hence the action is strictly relative. For we should remember that *rising* and *setting, up* and *down, above* and *below,* in reference to the earth, are only relative terms.

We speak and read of the *changes* of the moon, and we correctly understand each other. But in truth the moon changes no more at one time than at another. The action is purely relative. One day we observe it *before* the sun, and the next *behind* it, as we understand these terms. The precise time of the change, when it will appear to us in a different relation to the sun, is computed by astronomers, and set down in our almanacs; but it changes no more at that time than at any other, for like every thing else, it is *always changing.*

In a case we mentioned in a former lecture, "John *looks* like or *resembles* his brother," we have an example of relative action. So in the case of two men travelling the same way, starting together, but advancing at different rates; one, we say, *falls* behind the other. In this manner of expression, we follow exactly the principles on which we started, and suit our language to our ideas and habits of thinking. By the law of optics things are reflected upon the retina of the eye inversely, that is, upside down; but they are always seen in a proper relation to each other, and if there is any thing wrong in the case, it is overcome by early habit; and so our language accords with things as they are manifested to our understandings.

These examples will serve to illustrate what we mean by relative action, when applied to natural philosophy or the construction of language.

I had intended in this lecture to have treated of the agents and objects of verbs, to prove, in accordance with the first and closest principles of philosophy, that every "*cause* must have an *effect,*" or, in other words, that every action must terminate on some object, either expressed or necessarily understood; but I am admonished that I have occupied more than my usual quota of time in this lecture already, and hence I shall leave this work for our next.

I will conclude by the relation of an anecdote or two from the life of that wonderful man, Gallileo Gallilei, who was many years professor of mathematics at Padua. Possessed of a strong, reflecting mind, he had early given his attention to the observation of things, their motions, tendencies, and power of resistance, from which he ascended, step by step, to the sublime science of astronomy. Being of an honest and frank, as well as benevolent disposition, he shunned not to state and defend theories at war with the then received opinions. All learning was, at that time, in the hands or under the supervision of the ecclesiastics, who were content to follow blindly the aristotelian philosophy, which, in many respects, was not unlike that still embraced in our *neuter verb systems* of grammar. There was a sworn hostility against all improvement, or innovation as it was called, in science as well as in theology. The copernican system, to which Gallileo was inclined, if it had not been formally condemned, had been virtually denounced as false, and its advocates heretical. Hence Gallileo never dared openly to defend it, but, piece by piece, under different names, he brought it forth, which, carried out, would establish the heretical system. Dwelling as a light in the midst of surrounding darkness, he cautiously discovered the precious truths revealed to his mind, lest the flood of light should distract and destroy the mental vision, break up the elements of society, let loose the resistless powers of ignorance, prejudice and bigotry, and envelope himself and friends in a common ruin. At length having prepared in a very guarded manner his famous "Dialogues on the Ptolmaic and Copernican Systems," he obtained permission, and ventured to publish it to the world, altho an edict had been promulgated enjoining silence on the subject, and he had been personally instructed "*not to believe or teach the motion of the earth in any manner*."

By the false representation of his enemies, suspicions were aroused and busily circulated prejudicial to Gallileo. Pope Urban himself, his former friend, became exasperated towards him, and a sentence against him and his books was fulminated by the Cardinals, prohibiting the "sale and vending of the latter, and condemning him to the formal prison of the Holy Office for a period determined at their pleasure." The sentence of the Inquisition was in part couched in these words—"We pronounce, judge, and declare, that you, the said Gallileo, by reason of these things, which have been detailed in the course of this investigation, and which, as above, you have confessed, have rendered yourself vehemently suspected by this Holy Office, of heresy; that is to say, that you believe and hold the false doctrine, and contrary to the Holy and Divine Scriptures, namely, that the sun is the center of the world, and that it does not *move* from east to west, and that the earth does *move*, and is not the center of the world; also, that an opinion *can be held* and *supported* as *probable, after it has been* declared, and finally decreed contrary to the Holy Scriptures"—by the Holy See!! "From which," they continue, "it is *our* pleasure that you be absolved, provided that, first, with a *sincere* heart, and *unfeigned faith*, in our presence, you *abjure, curse*, and *detest* the said errors and heresies, and every other error and heresy contrary to the Catholic and Apostolic Church of Rome, in the form now shown to you."

After suffering under this anathema some time, Gallileo, by the advice of his friends, consented to make a public abjuration of his former heresies on the laws of motion. Kneeling before the "Most Eminent and Most Reverend Lords Cardinals, General Inquisitors of the universal Christian republic, against *heretical depravity*, having before his eyes the Holy Gospels," he swears that he always "*believed*, and now *believes*, and with the help of God, *will in future believe*, every article which the Holy Catholic Church of Rome holds, teaches, and preaches"—that he does altogether "abandon the false opinion which maintains that the 'sun is the center of the world, and that the earth is *not* the center and *movable*,' that with a sincere heart and unfeigned faith, he abjures, curses, and detests the said errors and heresies, and every other error and sect contrary to the said Holy Church, and that he will never more in future, say or assert any thing verbally, or in writing, which may give rise to similar suspicion." As he arose from his knees, it is said, he whispered to a friend standing near him, "*E pur si muove*"—IT DOES MOVE, THO.

In our times we are not fated to live under the terrors of the Inquisition; but prejudice, if not as strong in power to execute, has the ability to blind as truly as in other ages, and keep us from the knowledge and adoption of practical improvements. And it is the same philosophy now, which *asks* if *inanimate matter can act*, which *demanded* of Gallileo if this ponderous globe could fly a thousand miles in a minute, and no body feel the motion; and with Deacon Homespun, in the dialogue, "why, if this world turned upside down, the water did not spill from the mill ponds, and all the people fall headlong to the bottomless pit?"

If there are any such peripatetics in these days of light and science, who still cling to the false and degrading systems of neutrality, because they are honorable for age, or sustained by learned and good men, and who will oppose all improvement, reject without examination, or, what is still worse, refuse to adopt, after being convinced of the truth of it, any system, because it is novel, an innovation upon established forms, I can only say of them, in the language of Micanzio, the Venetian friend of Gallileo—"The efforts of such enemies to get these principles prohibited, will occasion no loss either to your reputation, or to the intelligent part of the world. As to posterity, this is just one of the surest ways to hand them down to them. But what a wretched set this must be, to whom every good thing, and *all that is found in nature*, necessarily appears hostile and odious."

A philosophical axiom. — Manner of expressing action. — Things taken for granted. — Simple facts must be known. — Must never deviate from the truth. — Every *cause* will have an *effect*. — An example of an intransitive verb. — Objects expressed or implied. — All language eliptical. — Intransitive verbs examined. — I run. — I walk. — To step. — Birds fly. — It rains. — The fire burns. — The sun shines. — To smile. — Eat and drink. — Miscellaneous examples. — Evils of false teaching. — A change is demanded. — These principles apply universally. — Their importance.

We have made some general remarks on the power, cause, and means, necessary in the production of action. We now approach nearer to the application of these principles as observed in the immediate *agency* and *effects* which precede and follow action, and as connected with the verb.

It is an axiom in philosophy which cannot be controverted, that every *effect* is the product of a prior *cause*, and that every *cause* will necessarily produce a corresponding *effect*. This fact has always existed and will forever remain unchanged. It applies universally in physical, mental, and moral science; to God or man; to angels or to atoms; in time or thro eternity. No language can be constructed which does not accord with it, for no ideas can be gained but by an observance of its manifestations in the material or spiritual universe. The manner of *expressing* this cause and effect may differ in different nations or by people of the same nation, but the fact remains unaltered, and so far as understood the idea is the same. In the case of the horse mentioned in a former lecture,[12] the idea was the same, but the manner of expressing it different. Let that horse *walk*, *lay* down, *roll* over, *rise* up, *shake* himself, *rear*, or *stand* still, all present will observe the same attitude of the horse, and will form the same ideas of his positions. Some will doubtless inquire more minutely into the *cause* and *means* by which these various actions are produced, what muscles are employed, what supports are rendered by the bones; and the whole regulated by the will of the horse, and their conclusions may be quite opposite. But this has nothing to do with the obvious fact expressed by the words above; or, more properly, it is not necessary to enter into a minute detail of these minor considerations, these secret springs of motion, in order to relate the actions of the horse. For were we to do this we should be required to go back, step by step, and find the causes still more numerous, latent, and perplexing. The pursuit of causes would lead us beyond the mere organization of the horse, his muscular energy, and voluntary action; for gravitation has no small service to perform in the accomplishment of these results; as well as other principles. Let gravitation be removed, and how could the horse *lay* down? He could *roll* over as well in the air as upon the ground. But the particular notice of these things is unnecessary in the construction of language to express the actions of the horse; for he stands as the obvious *agent* of the whole, and the *effects* are seen to follow—the *horse* is laid down, *his body* is rolled over, *the fore part* of it is *reared up, himself* is shaken, and the whole *feat* is produced by the direction of his master.

Allow me to recal an idea we considered in a former lecture. I said no action as such could be known distinct from the thing which acts; that action as such is not perceptible, and that all things act, according to the ability they possess. To illustrate this idea: Take a magnet and lower it down over a piece of iron, till it attracts it to itself and holds it suspended there. If you are not in possession of a magnet you can make one at your pleasure, by the following process. Lay your knife blade on a flat iron, or any hard, smooth surface; let another take the old tongs or other iron which have stood erect for a considerable length of time, and draw it upon the blade for a minute or more. A magnetic power will be conveyed from the tongs to the blade sufficient to take up a common needle. The tongs themselves may be manufactured into a most perfect magnet. Now as the knife *holds* the needle suspended beneath it you perceive there must be an action, a power, and cause exerted beyond our comprehension. Let the magnetic power be extracted from the blade, and the needle will drop to the floor. A common unmagnetized blade will not *raise* and *hold* a needle as this does. How those tongs come in possession of such astonishing power; by what process it is there retained; the power and means of transmission of a part of it to the knife blade, and the reason of the phenomena you now behold—an inanimate blade drawing to itself and there holding this needle suspended— will probably long remain unknown to mortals. But that such are the facts, incontestibly true, none will deny, for the evidence is before us. Now fix your attention on that needle. There is an active and *acting* principle in that as well as in the magnetized blade; for the blade will not attract a splinter of wood, of whalebone, or piece of glass, tho equal in size and weight. It will have no operation on them. Then it is by a sort of mutual affinity, a reciprocity of attachment, between the blade and needle, that this phenomena is produced.

To apply this illustration you have only to reverse the case—turn the knife and needle over—and see all things attracted to the earth by the law of gravitation, a principle abiding in all matter. All that renders the exhibition of the magnet curious or wonderful is that it is an uncommon condition of things, an apparent counteraction of the regular laws of nature. But we should know that the same sublime principle is constantly operating thro out universal nature. Let that be suspended, cease its active operations for a moment, and our own earth will be decomposed into particles; the sun, moon and stars will dissolve and mingle with the common dust; all creation will crumble into atoms, and one vast ocean of darkness and chaos will fill the immensity of space.

Are you then prepared to deny the principles for which we are contending? I think you will not; but accede the ground, that such being the fact, true in nature, language, correctly explained, is only the medium by which the ideas of these great truths, may be conveyed from one mind to another, and must correspond therewith. If language is the sign of ideas, and ideas are the impressions of things, it follows of necessity, that no language can be employed unless it corresponds with these natural laws, or first principles. The untutored child cannot talk of these things, nor comprehend our meaning till clearly explained to it. But some people act as tho they thought children must first acquire a knowledge of words, and then begin to learn what such words mean. This is putting the "cart before the horse."

Much, in this world, is to be taken for granted. We can not enter into the minutiæ of all we would express, or have understood. We go upon the ground that other people know something as well as we, and that they will exercise that knowledge while listening to our relation of some new and important facts. Hence it is said that "brevity is the soul of wit." But suppose you should talk of surds, simple and quadratic equations, diophantine problems, and logarithms, to a person who knows nothing of proportion or relation, addition or subtraction. What would they know about your words? You might as well give them a description in Arabic or Esquimaux. They must first learn the simple rules on which the whole science of mathematics depends, before they can comprehend a dissertation on the more abstruse principles or distant results. So children must learn to observe things as they are, in their simplest manifestations, in order to understand the more secret and sublime operations of nature. And our language should always be adapted to their capacities; that is, it should agree with their advancement. You may talk to a zealot in politics of religion, the qualities of forbearance, candor, and veracity; to the enthusiast of science and philosophy; to the bigot of liberality and improvement; to the miser of benevolence and suffering; to the profligate of industry and frugality; to the misanthrope of philanthropy and patriotism; to the degraded sinner of virtue, truth, and heaven; but what do they know of your meaning? How are they the wiser for your instruction? You have touched a cord which does not vibrate thro their hearts, or, phrenologically, addressed an organ they do not possess, except in a very moderate degree, at least. Food must be seasoned to the palates of those who use it. Milk is for babes and strong meat for men. Our instruction must be suited to the capacities of those we would benefit, always elevated just far enough above them to attract them along the upward course of improvement.

But it should be remembered that evils will only result from a deviation from truth, and that we can never be justified in doing wrong because others have, or for the sake of meeting them half way. And yet this very course is adopted in teaching, and children are learned to adopt certain technical rules in grammar, not because they are *true*, but because they are *convenient*! In fact, it is said by some, that language is an arbitrary affair altogether, and is only to be taught and learned mechanically! But who would teach children that *seven times seven* are *fifty*, and *nine times nine* a *hundred*, and assign as a reason for so doing, that *fifty* and a *hundred* are more easily remembered than *forty-nine* and *eighty-one*? Yet there would be as much propriety in adopting such a principle in mathematics, as in teaching for a rule of grammar that when an objective case comes after a verb, it is active; but when there is none expressed, it is intransitive or neuter.

The great fault is, grammarians do not allow themselves to *think* on the subject of language, or if they do, they only think intransitively, that is, produce no *thoughts* by their cogitations.

This brings us to a more direct consideration of the subject before us. All admit the correctness of the axiom that every effect must have a cause, and that every cause will have an effect. It is equally true that "*like causes will produce like effects*," a rule from which nature itself, and thought, and language, can never deviate. It is as plain as that two things mutually equal to each other, are equal to a third. On this immutable principle we base our theory of the activity of all verbs, and contend that they must have an object after them, either expressed or *necessarily understood*. We can not yield this position till it is proved that *causes* can operate without producing effects, which can never be till the order of creation is reversed! There never was, to our knowledge, such a thing as an intransitive action, with the solitary exception of the burning bush.[13] In that case the laws of nature were suspended, and no effects were produced; for the *bush burned*, but there was nothing burnt; no consequences followed to the bush; it was not consumed. The records of the past present no instance of like character, where effects have failed to follow, direct or more distantly, every cause which has been set in operation.

It makes no difference whether the object of the action is expressed or not. It is the same in either case. But where it is not necessarily implied from the nature and fitness of things, it must be expressed, and but for such object or effect the action could not be understood. For example, *I run*; but if there is no effect produced, *nothing* run, how can it be known whether I run or not. If I write, it is necessarily understood that I write *something*—a *letter*, a *book*, a *piece* of poetry, a *communication*, or some other *writing*. When such object is not liable to be mistaken, it would be superfluous to express it —it would be a redundancy which should be avoided by all good writers and speakers. All languages are, in this respect, more or less eliptical, which constitutes no small share of their beauty, power, and elegance.

This elipsis may be observed not only in regard to the objects of verbs, but in the omission of many nouns after adjectives, which thus assume the character of nouns; as, the Almighty, the Eternal, the Allwise, applied to God, understood. So we say the wise, the learned, the good, the faithful, the wicked, the vile, the base, to which, if nouns, it would sound rather harsh to apply plurals. So we say, take your hat off (   ); put your gloves on (   ); lay your coat off (   ); and pull your boots on (   ); presuming the person so addressed knows enough to fill the elipsis, and not take his hat off his back, pull his gloves on his feet, or his boots on his head.

In pursuing this subject farther, let us examine the sample words which are called *intransitive* verbs, because frequently used without the object expressed after them; such as run, walk, step, fly, rain, snow, burn, roll, shine, smiles, &c.

"*I run.*"

That here is an action of the first kind, none will deny. But it is contended by the old systems that there is no object on which the action terminates. If that be true then there is *nothing* run, no effect produced, and the first law of nature is outraged, in the very onset; for there is a *cause*, but no *effect*; an *action*, but no *object*. How is the fact? Have you run nothing? conveyed nothing, moved nothing from one place to another? no change, no effect, nothing moved? Look at it and decide. It is said that a neuter or intransitive verb may be known from the fact that it takes after it a preposition. Try it by this rule. "A man run *against* a post in a dark night, and broke his neck;" that is, he run nothing against a post—no object to run—and yet he broke his neck. Unfortunate man!

The fact in relation to this verb is briefly this: It is used to express the action which more usually terminates on the actor, than on any other object. This circumstance being generally known, it would be superfluous to mention the object, except in cases where such is not the fact. But whenever we desire to be definite, or when there is the least liability to mistake the object, it is invariably expressed. Instances of this kind are numerous. "They *ran* the *boat* ashore." "The captain *ran* his *men* to rescue them from the enemy." "They *ran* the *gauntlet*." "They *run* a *stage* to Boston." "He *ran* himself into discredit." "One bank *runs* another." "The man had a hard *run* of it." "*Run* the *account* over, and see if it is right." "They *run forty looms* and two thousand spindles." "He *runs* his *mill* evenings." Such expressions are common and correct, because they convey ideas, and are understood.

Two men were engaged in argument. The believer in intransitive verbs set out to *run his opponent* into an evident absurdity, and, contrary to his expectation, he *ran himself* into one. Leave out the objects of this verb, run, and the sense is totally changed. He set out to *run* into an *evident absurdity*, and he ran into one; that is, he did the very absurd thing which he intended to do.[14]

"*I walk.*"

The action expressed by this verb is very similar in character to the former, but rather *slower* in performance. Writers on health tell us that *to walk* is a very healthy exercise, and that it would be well for men of sedentary habits *to walk* several miles every day. But if there is no action in walk, or if it has no *object* necessarily *walked*, it would be difficult to understand what good could result from it.

"Did you have a pleasant *walk* this morning?" says a teacher to his grammar class.

"We did have a very pleasant one. The flowers were *blooming* on each side of the *walk*, and *sent* forth their sweetest aroma, *perfuming* the soft breezes of the morning. Birds were *flitting from* spray to spray, *carolling* their hymns of praise to Deity. The tranquil waters of the lake lay *slumbering* in silence, and *reflected* the bright *rays* of the sun, *giving* a sweet but solemn *aspect* to the whole scene. *To go* thro the grove, down by the lake, and up thro the meadow, is the most delightful *walk* a person can take."

"How did you get your *walk*?"

"We walked it, to be sure; how did you think we got it?"

"Oh, I did not know. *Walk*, your books tell you, is an intransitive verb, terminating on no object; so I supposed, if you followed them, you obtained it some other way; by *riding, running, sailing*, or, may be, *bought* it, as you could not have *walked it*! Were you tired on your return?"

"We were exceedingly fatigued, for you know it is a very long *walk*, and we *walked it* in an hour."

"But *what* tired you? If there are no effects produced by walking, I can not conceive why *you* should be fatigued by such exercise."

Who does not perceive what flagrant violations of grammar rules are committed every day, and every hour, and in almost every sentence that is framed to express our knowledge of facts.

To step.

This verb is the same in character with the two just noticed. It expresses the act of *raising* each foot alternately, and usually implies that the body is, by that means, conveyed from one place to another. But as people *step* their *feet* and not their hands, or any thing else, it is entirely useless to mention the object; for generally, that can not be mistaken any more than in the case of the gloves, boots, and hat. But it would be bad philosophy to teach children that there is no objective word after it, because it is not written out and placed before their eyes. They will find such teaching contradicted at every *step* they take. Let a believer in intransitive verbs *step* on a red hot iron; he will soon find to his sorrow, that he was mistaken when he thought that he could *step* without stepping any thing. It would be well for grammar, as well as many other things, to have more practice and less theory. The thief was detected by his steps. Step softly; put your feet down carefully.

Birds fly.

We learned from our primers, that

> "The eagle's *flight*
> Is out of sight,"

How did the eagle succeed in producing a *flight*? I suppose he *flew* it. And if birds ever fly, they must produce a flight. Such being the fact, it is needless to supply the object. But the action does not terminate solely on the flight produced, for that is only the name given to the action itself. The expression conveys to the mind the obvious fact, that, by strong muscular energy, by the aid of feathers, and the atmosphere, the bird carries itself thro the air, and changes its being from one place to another. As birds rarely fly a race, or any thing but *themselves* and a *flight*, it is not necessary to suffix the object.

It rains.

This verb is insisted on as the strongest proof of intransitive action; with what propriety, we will now inquire. It will serve as a clear elucidation of the whole theory of intransitive verbs.

What does the expression signify? It simply declares the fact, that *water is shed* down from the clouds. But is there no object after *rains*? There is none expressed. Is there nothing rained? no effect produced? If not, there can be no water fallen, and our cisterns would be as empty, our streams as low, and fields as parched, after a rain as before it! But who that has common sense, and has never been blinded by the false rules of grammar, does not know that when *it rains*, it never fails to *rain rain, water,* or *rain-water*, unless you have one of the paddy's dry rains? When it hails, it hails *hail, hail-stones*, or frozen *rain*. When it snows, it *snows snow*, sometimes two feet of it, sometimes less. I should think teachers in our northern countries would find it exceeding difficult to convince their readers that snow is an intransitive verb—that it snows *nothing*. And yet so it is; people will remain wedded to their old systems, and refuse to open their eyes and behold the evidences every where around them. Teachers themselves, the guides of the young—and I blush to say it, for I was long among the number—have, with their scholars, labored all the morning, breaking roads, *shovelling snow*, and clearing paths, to get to the school-house, and then set down and taught them that *to snow* is an *in*transitive verb. What nonsense; nay, worse, what falsehoods have been instilled into the youthful mind in the name of grammar! Can we be surprised that people have not understood grammar? that it is a dry, cold, and lifeless business?

I once lectured in Poughkeepsie, N. Y. In a conversation with Miss B., a distinguished scholar, who had taught a popular female school for twenty years; was remarking upon the subject of intransitive verbs, and the apparent inconsistency of the new system, that all verbs must have an object after them, expressed or understood; she said, "there was the verb *rain*, (it happened to be a rainy day,) the whole action is confined to the agent; it does not pass on to another object; it is purely intransitive." Her aged mother, who had never looked into a grammar book, heard the conversation, and very bluntly remarked, "Why, you fool you, I want to know if you have studied grammar these thirty years, and taught it more than twenty, and have never *larned* that when it rains it *always* rains *rain*? If it didn't, do you s'pose you'd need an umbrella to go out now into the storm? I should think you'd know better. I always told you these plaguy grammars were good for nothing, I didn't b'lieve." "Amen," said I, to the good sense of the old lady, "you are right, and have reason to be thankful that you have never been initiated into the intricate windings, nor been perplexed with the false and contradictory rules, which have blasted many bright geniuses in their earliest attempts to gain a true knowledge of the sublime principles of language, on which depends so much of the happiness of human life." The good matron's remark was a poser to the daughter, but it served as a means of her entire deliverance from the thraldom of neuter verbs, and the adoption of the new principles of the exposition of language.

The anecdote shows us how the unsophisticated mind will observe facts, and employ words as correctly, if not more so, than those schooled in the high pretensions of science, falsely taught. Who does not know from the commonest experience, that the direct object of *raining* must follow as the necessary sequence? that it can never fail? And yet our philologists tell us that such is not always the case; and that the exception is to be marked on the singular ground, whether the word is written out or omitted! What a narrow view of the sublime laws of motion! What a limited knowledge of things! or else, what a *mistake*!

"Then the Lord said unto Moses, behold, I will *rain* bread for you from heaven."

"Then the *Lord rained* down, upon Sodom and Gomorrah, *brimstone* and *fire*, from the Lord out of heaven."—*Bible.*

The fire burns.

The fire *burns* the wood, the coal, or the peat. The great fire in New-York *burned* the buildings which covered fifty-two acres of ground. Mr. Experiment *burns* coal in preference to wood. His new grate *burns it* very finely. Red ash coal *burns* the best; it *makes* the fewest *ashes*, and hence *is* the most convenient. The cook *burns* too much fuel. The house took fire and *burned* up. *Burned what* up? Burn is an intransitive verb. It would not trouble the unfortunate tenant to know that there must be an *object burned*, or what *it* was. He would find it far more difficult to rebuild his *house*. Do you suppose fires never burn any thing belonging to neuter verb folks? Then they never need pay away insurance money. With the solitary exception I have mentioned—the burning bush—this verb can not be intransitive.

The sun shines.

This is an intransitive verb if there ever was one, because the object is not often expressed after it. But if the sun *emits* no *rays* of light, how shall it be known whether it shines or not? "The *radiance* of the sun's bright beaming" is produced by the *exhibition* of *itself,* when it *brightens* the objects exposed to its *rays* or *radiance.* We talk of *sun shine* and moon shine, but if these bodies never produce *effects* how shall it be known whether such things are real? *Sun shine* is the direct effect of the sun's *shining.* But clouds sometimes intervene and prevent the rays from extending to the earth; but *then* we do not say "the sun *shines.*" You see at once, that all we know or can know of the fact we state as truth, is derived from a knowledge of the very *effects* which our grammars tell us do not exist. Strange logic indeed! It is a mark of a wiser man, and a better scholar, not to know the popular grammars, than it is to profess any degree of proficiency in them!

To smile.

The *smiles* of the morning, the *smiles* of affection, a *smile* of kindness, are only produced by the appearance of something that *smiles* upon us. *Smiles* are the direct consequence of *smiling.* If a person should *smile* ever so *sweetly* and yet present no *smiles,* they might, for aught we could know to the contrary, be *sour* as vinegar.

But this verb frequently has another object after it; as, "to *smile* the *wrinkles* from the brow of age," or "*smile* dull *cares* away." "A sensible wife would soon *reason* and *smile him* into good nature."

But I need not multiply examples. When such men as Johnson, Walker, Webster, Murray, Lowthe, and a host of other wise and renowned men, gravely tell us that *eat* and *drink,* which they define, "to *take food; to feed; to take a meal; to go to meals;* to be maintained in food; *to swallow liquors; to quench thirst;* to take any liquid;" are *intransitive* or *neuter* verbs, having no objects after them, we must think them insincere, egregiously mistaken, or else possessed of a means of subsistence different from people generally! Did they *eat* and *drink,* "take food and swallow liquors," *in*transitively; that is, without *eating* or *drinking* any thing? Is it possible in the nature of things? Who does not see the absurdity? And yet they were *great* men, and nobody has a right to question such *high* authority. And the "*simplifiers*" who have come after, making books and teaching grammar to *earn* their *bread*, have followed close in their footsteps, and, I suppose, *eaten* nothing, and thrown their bread away! Was I a believer in neuter verbs and desired to get money, my first step would be to set up a boarding house for all believers in, and *practisers* of, intransitive verbs. I would board cheap and give good fare. I could afford it, for no provisions would be consumed.

Some over cautious minds, who are always second, if not last, in a good cause, ask us why these principles, if so true and clear, were not found out before? Why have not the learned who have studied for many centuries, never seen and adopted them? It is a sufficient answer to such a question, to ask why the copernican system of astronomy was not sooner adopted, why the principles of chemistry, the circulation of the blood, the power and application of steam, nay, why all improvement was not known before. When grammar and dictionary makers, those wise expounders of the principles of speech, have so far forgotten facts as to teach that *eat* and *drink*, "express neither action nor passion," or are "confined to the agents;" that when a man eats, he eats nothing, or when he drinks, he drinks nothing, we need not stop long to decide why these things were unknown before. The wisest may sometimes mistake; and the proud aspirant for success, frequently passes over, unobserved, the humble means on which all true success depends.

Allow me to quote some miscellaneous examples which will serve to show more clearly the importance of supplying the elipses, in order to comprehend the meaning of the writers, or profit by their remarks. You will supply the objects correctly from the attendant circumstances where they are not expressed.

"Ask (   ) and ye shall receive (   ); seek (   ) and ye shall find (   ); knock (   ) and *it* shall be opened unto you."

Ask *what*? Seek *what*? Knock *what*? That *it* may be opened? Our "Grammars Made Easy" would teach us to *ask* and *seek* nothing! no objectives after them. What then could we reasonably expect to *receive* or *find*? The *thing* we *asked* for, of course, and that was nothing! Well might the language apply to such, "Ye ask ( ) and *receive not* (naught) because ye ask ( ) amiss." False teaching is as pernicious to religion and morals as to science.

"Charge them that are rich in this world—that they *do good*, that they be rich in good works, ready to *distribute* ( ), willing to *communicate* ( )."—*Paul to Timothy.*

The hearer is to observe that there is no object after these words—*nothing* distributed, or communicated! There is too much such charity in the world.

"He spoke ( ), and *it* was done; he commanded ( ), and *it* stood fast."

"*Bless* ( ), and *curse* ( ) not."—*Bible.*

"*Strike* ( ) while the iron is hot."—*Proverb.*

"I *came* ( ), I *saw* ( ), I *conquered* ( )."—*Cæsar's Letter.*

He lives ( ) contented and happy.

"The *life* that I now *live*, in the flesh, I *live* by the faith of the son of God."—*Paul.*

"Let me *die* the *death* of the righteous, and let my last *end be* like his."—*Numbers.*

As bodily exercise particularly strengthens ( ), as it invites ( ) to sleep ( ), and secures ( ) against great disorders, it is to be generally encouraged. Gymnastic exercises may be established for all ages and for all classes. The Jews were ordered to *take a walk* out of the city on the Sabbath day; and here rich and poor, young and old, master and slave, met ( ) and indulged ( ) in innocent mirth or in the pleasures of friendly intercourse.—*Spurzheim on Education.*

"Men will wrangle ( ) for religion; write ( ) for it; fight ( ) for it; die ( ) for it; any thing but live ( ) for it."—*Lacon.*

"I have addressed this volume to those that think ( ), and some may accuse me of an ostentatious independence, in presuming ( ) to inscribe a book to so small a minority. But a volume addressed to those that think ( ) is in fact addressed to all the world; for altho the proportion of those who *do* ( ) think ( ) be extremely small, yet every individual *flatters himself* that he is one of the number."—*Idem.*

What is the difference whether a man *thinks* or not, if he produces no *thoughts*?

"He that *thinks himself* the happiest man, really is so; but he that *thinks himself* the wisest, is generally the greatest fool."—*Idem.*

"A man *has* many *workmen employed*; some to plough ( ) and sow ( ), others to chop ( ) and split ( ); some to mow ( ) and reap ( ); one to score ( ) and hew ( ); two to frame ( ) and raise ( ). In his factory he has persons to card ( ), spin ( ), reel ( ), spool ( ), warp ( ), and weave ( ), and a clerk to deliver ( ) and charge ( ), to receive ( ) and pay ( ). They eat ( ), and drink ( ), heartily, three times a day; and as they work ( ) hard, and feel ( ) tired at night, they lay ( ) down, sleep ( ) soundly, and dream ( ) pleasantly; they rise ( ) up early to go ( ) to work ( ) again. In the morning the children wash ( ) and dress ( ) and prepare ( ) to go ( ) to school, to learn ( ) to read ( ), write ( ), and cipher ( )." All neuter or intransitive verbs!!

"The celebrated horse, Corydon, will perform ( ) on Tuesday evening in the circus. He will leap ( ) over four bars, separately, in imitation of the english hunter. He will lie ( ) down, and rise ( ) up instantly at the *word of command*. He will move ( ) backwards and sideways, rear ( ) and stand ( ) on his hind feet; he will sit ( ) down, like a Turk, on a cushion. To conclude ( ), he will leap ( ), in a surprising manner, over two horses."— *Cardell's Grammar.*

The gymnastic is not a mountebank; he palms off no legerdemain upon the public. He will stretch a line across the room, several feet from the floor, over which he will leap ( ) with surprising dexterity. He will stand ( ) on his head, balance, ( ) on one foot, and swing ( ) from side to side of the room; lay ( ) crosswise, and sideways; spring ( ) upon his feet; bound ( ) upon the floor; dance ( ) and keel ( ) over with out touching his hands. He will sing ( ), play ( ), and mimic ( ); look ( ) like a king, and act ( ) like a fool. He will laugh ( ) and cry ( ), as if real; roar ( ) like a lion, and chirp ( ) like a bird. To conclude ( ): He will do all this to an audience of neuter grammarians, without either "*action* or *passion*," all the while having a "*state of being*," motionless, in the center of the room!!

What a lie! say you. *A lie?* I hope you do not accuse *me* of lying. If there is any thing false in this matter it all *lies* in the quotation, at the conclusion, from the standard grammar. If that is false, whose fault is it? Not mine, certainly. But what if I should *lie* (   ), intransitively? I should tell no falsehoods.

But enough of this. If there is any thing irrational or inconsistent, any thing false or ridiculous, in this view of the subject, it should be remembered that it has been long taught, not only in common schools, but in our academies and colleges, as serious, practical truth; as the only means of acquiring a correct knowledge of language, or fitting ourselves for usefulness or respectability in society. You smile at such trash, and well you may; but you must bear in mind that grammar is not the only thing in which we may turn round and *laugh* ( ) at past follies.

But I am disposed to consider this matter of more serious consequence than to deserve our *laughter*. When I see the rising generation spend months and years of the best and most important part of their lives, which should be devoted to the acquisition of that which is true and useful, studying the dark and false theory of language as usually taught, I am far from feeling any desire to laugh at the folly which imposes such a task upon them. I remember too distinctly the years that have just gone by. I have seen too many blighted hopes, too many wearisome hours, too many sad countenances, too many broken resolutions; to say nothing of corporeal chastisements; to think it a small matter that children are erroneously taught the rudiments of language, because sanctioned by age, or great names. A change, an important change, a radical change, in this department of education, is imperiously demanded, and teachers must obey the call, and effect the change. There is a spirit abroad in the land which will not bow tamely and without complaint, to the unwarranted dictation of arbitrary, false, and contradictory rules, merely from respect to age. It demands reason, consistency and plainness; and yields assent only where they are found. And teachers, if they will not lead in the reformation, must be satisfied to follow after; for a reformation is loudly called for, and will be had. None are satisfied with existing grammars, which, in principle, are nearly alike. The seventy-three attempts to improve and simplify Murray, have only acted *intransitively*, and accomplished very little, if any good, save the employment given to printers, paper makers, and booksellers.

But I will not enlarge. We have little occasion to wonder at the errors and mistakes of grammar makers, when our lexicographers tell us for sober truth, that TO ACT, *to be in action, not to rest*, to be in *motion*, to *move*, is *v. n.* a verb neuter, signifying *no action*!! or *v. i.* verb intransitive, producing *no effects*; and that a "*neuter verb* EXPRESSES (active transitive verb) *a state of being*!! There are few minds capable of adopting such premises, and drawing therefrom conclusions which are rational or consistent. Truth is rarely elicted from error, beauty from deformity, or order from confusion. While, therefore, we allow the neuter systems to sink into forgetfulness, as they usually do as soon as we leave school and shut our books, let us throw the mantle of charity over those who have thoughtlessly (without *thinking thoughts*) and innocently lead us many months in dark and doleful wanderings, in paths of error and contradiction, mistaken for the road to knowledge and usefulness. But let us resolve to save ourselves and future generations from following the same unpleasant and unprofitable course, and endeavor to *reflect* the *light* which may *shine* upon our minds, to dispel the surrounding darkness, and secure the light and knowledge of truth to those who shall come after us.

Many philologists have undertaken to explain our language by the aid of foreign tongues. Because there are genitive cases, different kinds of verbs, six tenses, etc. in the Latin or Greek, the same distinctions should exist in our grammars. But this argument will not apply, admitting that other languages will not allow of the plan of exposition we have adopted, which we very seriously question, tho we have not time to go into that investigation. We believe that the principles we have adopted are capable of universal application; that what is action in England would be action in Greece, Rome, Turkey, and every where else; that "*like causes will produce like effects*" all the world over. It matters not by whom the action is seen, it is the same, and all who gather ideas therefrom will describe it as it appears to them, let them speak what language they may. But if they have no ideas to express, they need no language to speak. Monkeys, for aught I know to the contrary, can speak as well as we; but the reason they do not, is because they have nothing to say.

Let Maelzael's automaton chess-player be exhibited to a promiscuous multitude. They would all attempt a description of it, so far as they were able to gain a knowledge of its construction, each in his own language. Some might be unable to trace the *cause*, the moving *power*, thro all the curiously arranged *means*, to the *agent* who acted as prime mover to the whole affair. Others, less cautious in their conclusions, might think it a perpetual motion. Such would find a *first cause* short of the Creator, the great original of all things and actions; and thus violate the soundest principles of philosophy. Heaven has never left a vacuum where a new and *self* sustaining power may be set in operation independent of his ever-present supervision; and hence the long talked of *perpetual motion* is the vainest chimera which ever occupied the human brain. It may well appear as the opposite extreme of neuter verbs; for, while one would give no action to matter according to the physical laws which regulate the world, the other would make matter act of itself, independent of the Almighty. Be it ours to take a more rational and consistent stand; to view all things and beings as occupying a place duly prescribed by Infinite Wisdom, *acting* according to their several abilities, and subject to the regulation of the all-pervading laws which guide, preserve, and harmonize the whole.

If there is a subject which teaches us beyond controversy the existence of a Supreme Power, a Universal Father, an all-wise and ever-present God, it is found in the order and harmony of all things, produced by the regulation of Divine laws; and man's superiority to the rest of the world is most clearly proved, from the possession of a power to adapt language to the communication of ideas in free and social converse, or in the transmission of thought, drawn from an observation and knowledge of things as presented to his understanding.

There is no science so directly important to the growth of intellect and the future happiness of the child, as the knowledge of language. Without it, what is life? Wherein would man be elevated above the brute? And what is language without ideas? A sound without harmony—a shadow without a substance.

Let language be taught on the principles of true philosophy, as a science, instead of an arbitrary, mechanical business, a mere art, and you will no longer hear the complaint of a "*dry, cold*, uninteresting study." Its rules will be simple, plain, and easy; and at every step the child will increase in the knowledge of more than *words*, in an acquaintance with principles of natural and moral science. And if there is any thing that will carry the mind of the child above the low and grovelling things of earth, and fill the soul with reverence and devotion to the Holy Being who fills immensity with his presence, it is when, from observing the laws which govern matter, he passes to observe the powers and capabilities of the mind, and thence ascends to the Intellectual Source of *light, life*, and *being*, and contemplates the perennial and ecstatic joys which flow from the presence of Deity; soul mingling with soul, love absorbed in love, and God all in all.

LECTURE XI.

ON VERBS.

The verb TO BE. — Compounded of different radical words. — AM. — Defined. — The name of Deity. — *Ei.* — Is. — ARE. — WERE, WAS. — BE. — A dialogue. — Examples. — Passive Verbs examined. — Cannot be in the present tense. — The past participle is an adjective.

We have gone through the examination of *neuter* and *intransitive* verbs, with the exception of the verb TO BE, which we propose to notice in this place. Much more might be said on the subjects I have discussed, and many more examples given to illustrate the nature and operation of actions as expressed by verbs, and also in reference to the *objects* of action; but I trust the hints I have given will be satisfactory. I am confident, if you will allow your minds to *think* correct *thoughts*, and not *suffer* them *to be* misled by erroneous teaching, you will arrive at the same conclusion that I have, viz. that all verbs depend on a *common principle* for their explanation; that they are alike active, and necessarily take an object after them, either expressed or understood, in accordance with the immutable law of nature, which teaches that like causes will produce like effects.

The verb TO BE, as it is called, is conjugated by the aid of six different words, in its various modes and tenses; *am, is, are, was, were, be. Am* is unchanged, always in the indicative mood, present tense, agreeing with the *first* person singular. *Is* is also unchanged, in the same mood and tense, agreeing with the *third* person singular. *Art*, in the singular, is the same as *are* in the plural. *Was* and *wast,* are the same as *were* and *wert* in meaning, being derived from the same etymon. *Be, being,* and *been,* are changes of the same word. *Be* was formerly extensively used in the indicative present, but in that condition it is nearly obsolete. *Were* was also used in the singular as well as plural, especially when coming before the agent; as, "were I to go, I would do your business." But it is now more common to have *was* correctly used in that case. But, as one extreme often follows another, people have laid *were* quite too much aside, and often crowd *was* into its place in common conversation; as "we *was* (were) there yesterday." "There *was* (were) five or six men engaged in the business." This error appears to be gaining ground, and should be checked before it goes farther.

The combination of these different words was produced by habit, to avoid the monotony which the frequent recurrence of one word, so necessary in the expression of thought, would occasion: the same as the past tense of *go* is made by the substitution of another word radically different, *went*, the past tense of *wend* or *wind*. "O'er hills and dales they *wend* their way." "The lowing herd *wind* slowly o'er the lea." *Go* and *wend* convey to our minds nearly the same ideas. The latter is a little more poetical, because less used. But originally their signification was quite different. So with the parts of the verb TO BE. They were consolidated as a matter of convenience, and now appear in their respective positions to express the idea of being, life, or existence.

I have said this verb expresses the highest degree of action. I will now attempt to prove it. I should like to go into a labored and critical examination of the words, and trace their changes thro various languages, was it in accordance with the design of these lectures. But as it is not, I shall content myself with general observations.

I am.

This word is not defined in our dictionaries. It is only said to be "*the first person of to be.*" We must look for its meaning some where else. It is a compound of two ancient words, *ah*, breath, to *breathe*, life, to *live*, light, to *light*; and *ma*, the *hand*, or to *hand*. It signifies to *vivify*, *sustain*, or *support* one's self in being or existence. In process of time, like other things in this mutable world, its form was changed, but the meaning retained. But as one person could not *vivify* or *live* another, *inflate* another's lungs, or breathe another's breath, it became restricted to the first person. It means, I *breathe breath*, *vivify myself*, *live life*, or *exercise* the power of *being* or *living*. It conveys this fact in every instance, for no person incapable of breathing can say *I am*. Let any person pronounce the word *ah-ma,* and they will at once perceive the appropriateness of the meaning here given. It is very similar to the letter *h,* and the pronoun, (originally *noun,*) *he,* or the "*rough breathing*" in the Greek language. *Ma* is compounded with many words which express action done by the hand; as, *ma*nufacture, *ma*numit. It denoted any action or work done by the hand as the instrument; but, like other words, it gradually changed its import, so as to express any *effective* operation. Hence the union of the words was natural and easy, and *ahma* denoted *breathing, to live* or sustain life. *H* is a precarious letter in all languages that use it, as the pronunciation of it by many who speak the English language, will prove. It was long ago dropt, in this word, and after it the last *a,* so that we now have the plain word *am.*

It was formerly used as a noun in our language, and as such may be found in Exodus 3: 13, 14. "And Moses said unto God, Behold when I come unto the children of Israel and shall say unto them, The God of your fathers sent me unto you; and they shall say to me, What is his *name*? what shall I say unto them? And God said unto Moses, I AM the I AM; and he said, Thus shalt thou say unto the children of Israel, I AM hath sent me unto you." Chap. 6: 3.—"I appeared unto Abraham, unto Isaac, and unto Jacob, by the name of God Almighty; but by my name JEHOVAH (I AM) was I not known unto them." The word *Jehovah* is the same as *am.* It is the name of the *self-existent, self-sustaining* BEING, who has not only power to uphold all things, but to perform the still more sublime action of *upholding* or *sustaining himself.* This is the highest possible degree of action. Let this fail, and all creation will be a wreck. He is the *ever-living, uncontrolled, unfailing, unassisted,* and *never-changing* God, the Creator, Preserver, Alpha and Omega, the Beginning and End of all things. He is the *First Cause* of all causes, the *Agent,* original moving Power, and guiding Wisdom, which set in motion the wheels of universal nature, and guides and governs them without "variableness or the shadow of turning."

"I AM the first, and I, the last,
    Thro endless years the same;
I AM is my memorial still,
    And my eternal name."

Watts' Hymn.

Ask the Jews the meaning of this *neuter verb* in their language. They hold it in the most profound and superstitious reverence. After the captivity of their nation they never dared pronounce the name except once a year when the high priest went into the Holy of Holies, and hence the true pronunciation of it was lost. Unto this day they dare not attempt to utter it. In all their writings it remains in characters untranslated. When their Messiah comes they expect he will restore the pronunciation, and by it they shall be able to accomplish all things.[15]

According to Plutarch the Greeks had the letters EI, THOU ART, engraven on the temple of Apollo at Delphi, which is the second person of EIMI, *I am.*[16]

This motto was doubtless borrowed from the Jews, to whom it was given as the name of the God of Jacob. The same name you may see engraven on monuments, on pictures of the bible, on masonic implements, and in various places, untranslated.

Who can suppose that this word "expresses no action," when the very person incapable of it can not utter it, and no one else can speak it for him? It denotes the highest conceivable action applied to Deity or to man, and it is questionable philosophy which dares contradict this fact. The action expressed by it, is not changed, because it does not terminate on a foreign object. It remains the same. It is self-action.

He is.

This word is constructed from an old verb signifying *to stand forth, to appear, to show one's self,* and may be traced, I think, to the latin *eo, to go,* and *exist,* to *exeo, to go from*; that is, our *being* or *existence, came* or *stood forth* from God. It is certainly a contraction from the old english *to exist. Ist* is the spelling still retained in the german and some other languages. It denotes self-action. One man does not *exist* another, but himself. He *keeps himself* in existence.

We are, thou are-est, arst, or *art*.

Be not surprised when I tell you this is the same word as *air*, for such is the fact. It signifies to inhale air, to *air ourselves*, or *breathe air*. "God *breathed* into man the *breath of life*, and man became a *living soul*." The new born infant *inhales air, inflates its lungs* with *air*, and begins to live. We all know how essential *air* is to the preservation of life. No animal can live an instant without it. Drop a squirrel into a receiver from which all *air* has been extracted, and it can not live. Even vegetables will die where there is no air. *Light* is also indispensable to *life* and *health*. *Air* is *inhaled* and *exhaled*, and from it life receives support. The fact being common, it is not so distinctly observed by the careless, as tho it was more rare. But did you never see the man dying of a consumption, when the pulmonary or breathing organs were nearly decayed? How he labors for breath! He asks to have the windows thrown open. At length he *suffocates* and dies. Most persons struggle hard for *breath* in the hour of dissolving nature. The heaving bosom, the hollow gasp for *air*, tells us that the lamp of life is soon to be extinguished, that the hour of their departure has come.

When a person faints, we carry them into the *air*, or blow *air* upon them, that nature may be restored to its regular course. In certain cases physicians find it necessary to force air into the lungs of infants; they can after that *air*, themselves, *imbibe* or *drink in air*, or *inspirit* themselves with air. But I need not enlarge. Whoever has been deprived of air and labored hard for breath in a stifled or unwholesome air, can appreciate what we mean.

We were; he was.

I have said before that these words are the same, and are used in certain cases irrespective of number. I have good authority for this opinion, altho some etymologists give them different derivations.

Were, wert; worth, werth; word and *werde*, are derived from the same etymon and retain a similarity of meaning. They signify *spirit, life, energy*. "In the beginning was the *word*, and the *word* was with God." "By the *word* of his grace."

"*They were,*" they *inspirited* themselves, *possessed* the life, vitality, or *spirit,* the Creator gave them, and having that spirit, life, or energy, under proper regulation, in due degree, they were *worthy* of the esteem, regard, sympathy, and good *word* of others.

To be.

This is considered the root of all the words we have considered, and to it all others are referred for a definition. Dictionaries give no definition to *am, is, are, was,* and *were,* all of them as truly principal verbs as *be,* and possessed of as distinct a meaning. It can hardly be possible that they should form so important a part of our language, and yet be incapable of definition. But such is the fact, the most significant words in our language, and those most frequently used, are undefined in the books.

Mr. Webster says TO BE signifies, "to exist, to *have* a real *state* or *existence,*" and so say Walker and Johnson. Now if it is possible to "HAVE *a state of being* without action or passion," then may this word express neutrality. But the very definition requires activity, and an object expressed. It denotes the *act of being,* or living; to *exercise* the powers of life, to *maintain* a position or rank in the scale of existent things.

The name of the action is *being,* and applies to the Almighty BEING who *exists* unchanged as the source of all inferior *beings* and things, whose name is *Jehovah,* I AM, the Being of beings, the Fountain of *light, life,* and *wisdom.*

Be is used in the imperative and infinitive moods correctly, by every body who employs language. "*Be* here in ten minutes." "*Be it* far from thee." "I will *be* in Boston before noon." If there is any action in going from Providence to Boston at rail-road speed, in two hours, or before noon, it is all expressed by the verb *be,* which we are told expresses *no action.*

The teacher says to his scholars when out at play, "I want you *to be* in your seats in five minutes." What would they understand him to mean? that they should stand still? or that they should *change their state of being* from play in the yard, to a state of being in their seats? There is no word to denote such change, except the word *to be. Be* off, *be* gone, *be* here, *be* there, are commands frequently given and correctly understood.

The master says to a bright little lad, who has well learned his grammar, "*Be* here in a minute."

"Yes, sir, I will *be* there;" but he does not move.

"*Be* here immediately."

"Yes, yes, I will *be* there."

"Don't you understand me? I say, *be* here instantly."

"Oh, yes, I understand you and will obey."

The good man is enraged. "You scoundrel," says he, "do you mean to disobey my orders and insult me?"

"Insult you and disobey you; I have done neither," replies the honest boy.

"Yes you have, and I will chastise you severely for it."

"No, master, I have not; I declare, I have not. I have obeyed you as well as I know how, to the very letter and spirit of your command."

"Didn't I tell you *to be* here in a minute, and have not you *remained* where you were? and didn't you say you would *be* here?"

"Yes, sir; and did not I do just what you told me to?"

"Why, no, you blockhead; I told you *to be* here."

"Well, I told you I would *be* there."

"You *was* not here."

"Nor did you expect I would *be*, if you have taught me to *speak*, *write*, and understand correctly."

"What do you mean, you saucy boy?"

"I mean to mind my master, and do what he tells me to."

"Why didn't you do so then?"

"I did."

"You didn't."

"I did."

"You lie, you insult me, you contradict me, you saucy fellow. You are not fit to be in school. I will punish you severely." And in a passion he starts for his ferrule, takes the boys hand, and bruises him badly; the honest little fellow all the while pleading innocence of any intended wrong.

In a short time they commence *parsing* this sentence: "It is necessary *to be* very particular in ascertaining the meaning of words before we use them." The master puts *to be* to the same boy. He says it is an *active verb*, infinitive mood.

"How is that? an *active* verb?"

"Yes, sir."

"No, it is not. It is a *neuter* verb."

"Begging your pardon, master, it is not. It is active."

"Have I got to punish you again so soon, you impudent fellow. You are not fit to be in school. I will inform your parents of your conduct."

"What have I done that is wrong?"

"You say *to be* is an *active* verb, when *I* tell you, and the *grammar* and *dictionary* tell you, it is *neuter*!"

"What is a *neuter* verb, master?"

"It expresses 'neither action nor passion, but being or a state of being.' Have you forgotten it?"

"No, sir, I *thought* that was the case."

"What did you ask me for then?"

"Because I supposed you had found another meaning for it."

"To what do you allude, you troublesome fellow, you? I'll not bear your insults much longer."

"For what did you punish me so severely just now?"

"For disobeying my orders."

"What did you order me to do?"

"*To be* here in a minute."

"Well, did not I do what you told me?"

"No; you kept your seat, and did not come near me."

"Well, I thought and did just what you now tell me; that *to be* is a *neuter* verb, expressing no *action*, but *being*. I had a *state* of *being*, and promised to keep it, and did keep it, and you punished me for doing the very thing you told me to do!!"

The master looked down, shut up his book, and began to say that grammar is a "*dry, cold,* and *useless*" study, hardly worth the trouble of learning it.

"*I am* Alpha and Omega, the beginning and the ending, saith the Lord, who *is*, and who *was*, and who *is* to come, the Almighty."—*Rev. 1: 8.*

If there is any action in maintaining eternal existence, by which all things were created and are upheld, it is expressed in the verbs *am, is,* and *was.*

God said, "Let there *be* light, and there *was* light;" or more properly rendered, "Light BE, and light WAS."

Was there no action in setting the sun, moon and stars in the firmament, and in causing them to *send* forth the rays of light to *dispel* the surrounding darkness? If there was, *be* and *was* denote that action.

"You are commanded TO BE and *appear* before the court of common pleas," etc. A heavy penalty is imposed upon those who fail to comply with this citation—for neglecting to do what is expressed by the *neuter verb* to *be.*

Such cases might be multiplied without number, where this verb is correctly used by all who employ language, and correctly understood by all who are capable of knowing the meaning of words. But I think you must all be convinced of the truth of our proposition, that all verbs express action, either *real* or *relative*; and in all cases have an object, expressed or necessarily implied, which stands as the *effect*, and an agent, as the cause of action: and hence that language, as a means for the communication of thought, does not deviate from the soundest principles of philosophy, but in all cases, rightly explained, serves to illustrate them, in the plainest manner.

A few remarks on the "Passive Verb," and I will conclude this part of our subject, which has already occupied much more of our attention than I expected at the outset.

"*A verb passive* expresses a passion or a suffering, or the receiving of an action; and necessarily implies an object acted upon, and an agent by which it is acted upon; as, to be loved; Penelope is loved by me."

In the explanation of this verb, grammarians further tell us that a passive verb is formed by adding the verb *to be*, which is thus made auxiliary, to a past participle; as, Portia *was loved*. Pompey *was conquered*.

It is singular how forgetful our great men sometimes are about observing their own rules. Take an instance in Mr. Walker's octavo dictionary. Look for the word *simeter*, a small sword. You will find it spelled *scimitar*. Then turn over, and you will find it si*mita*r, with the same definition, and the remark, "more properly ci*meta*r." Then turn back, and find the correct word as he spells it, and there you will find it cime*te*r.

Unsettled as to the true spelling, go to our own honored Webster. Look for "scimiter." He says, see cimi*ta*r. Then look for "cimitar;" see cim*e*ter. Then hunt up the true word, be it *ar* or *er*, and you will find it still another way, cimi*te*r. Here the scholar has seven different ways to spell this word, and neither of his authorities have followed their own examples. I cite this as one of a thousand instances, where our savans have laid down rules for others, and disregarded them themselves.

Portia *is loved* and *happy*. She is *respectable, virtuous, talented*, and *respected* by all who know her. She *is seated by the door*. Does the *door* seat her? What agent, then, causes her *passion* or *suffering*?

The book is printed. Will you parse *is printed*? It is a passive verb, indicative mood, *present tense*. Who *is* printing it? causing it, in the present tense, to *suffer* or *receive* the action? The act of printing *was performed* a hundred years ago. How can it be present time?

Penelope *is loved* by me. The blow *is received* by me. It *is given* by me. Penelope *is seated* by me. The earthquake *is felt* by her. The evils *are suffered* by her. The thunder *is heard* by her. Does this mean that she is the agent, and the earthquake, evils, and thunder, are the objects which receive the *effects* which she produces? That would be singular philosophy, indeed. But *to feel*, *to suffer*, and *to hear*, are active, and are constructed into passive verbs. Why is it not as correct to say she *is suffering* by another's wrongs, *is raging* by the operation of passion, or *is travelling* by rail-road, are passive verbs? The fact is, our language can not *be explained* by set rules or forms of speech. We must regard the sense. The past participle, as it is called, becomes an adjective by use, and describes her as some way affected by a previous action. She is *learned, handsome, modest*, and, of course, *beloved* by all who know her.

To say "she *is placed* by the water's edge," is a passive verb, and that the water's edge, as the agent, causes her "passion, suffering, or receiving of the action," is false and ridiculous, for she *placed* herself there.

"We *are seated* on our seats by the stove." What power is *now* operating on us to make us suffer or receive the action of being seated on our seats? Does the stove perform this action? This is a passive verb, *present tense*, which requires an "object acted upon, and an *agent* by which it is acted upon." But we came in and *seated ourselves* here an hour ago.

The man *is acquitted*. He *stands acquitted* before the public. He *is learned*, wise, and happy, very much *improved* within a few years. He *is* always active, studious, and *engaged* in his own affairs. He *is renowned*, and *valorous*. She *is respected*. She *lives respected*.

If there is such a thing as a passive verb, it can never be used in the present tense, for the action expressed by the principal verb which is produced by the agent operating upon the object, is always *past* tense, and the auxiliary, or helping verb *to be*, is always present. Let this verb be analyzed, and the true meaning of each word understood, little difficulty will be found in giving it an explanation.

I will not spend more time in exposing the futility of this attempted distinction. It depends solely on a verbal form, but can never *be explained* so as *to be understood* by any scholar. Most grammarians have seen the fallacy of attempting to give the meaning of this verb. They can show its *form*, but *are* frequently *compelled*, as in the cases above, to sort out the "*passed* participles" from a host of adjectives, and it will *be found* exceeding troublesome to make scholars perceive any difference in the use of the words, or in the construction of a sentence. But it may be they have never thought that duty belonged to them; that they have nothing to do but to show them what the book says. Suppose they should teach arithmetic on the same principles, and learn the scholars to set down 144 as the product of 12 times 12. Let them look at the form of the figures, observe just how they appear, and make some more like them, and thus go thro the book. What would the child know of arithmetic? Just as much as they do of grammar, and no more. They would understand nothing of the science of numbers, of proportion, or addition. They would exercise the power of imitation, and make one figure look like another. Beyond that, all would be a *terra incognita*, a land unknown. So in the science of language; children may learn that the verb *to be*, joined with the past participle of an active verb, makes *a passive verb*; but what that passive verb is when made, or how to apply it, especially in the present tense, they have no means of knowing. Their knowledge is all taken on trust, and when thrown upon their own resources, they have none on which to rely.

LECTURE XII.

ON VERBS.

Mood. — Indicative. — Imperative. — Infinitive. — Former distinctions. — Subjunctive mood. — Time. — Past. — Present. — Future. — The future explained. — How formed. — Mr. Murray's distinction of time. — Imperfect. — Pluperfect. — Second future. — How many tenses. — Auxiliary Verbs. — Will. — Shall. — May. — Must. — Can. — Do. — Have.

We are now come to consider the different relations of action in reference to *manner* and *time*. We shall endeavor to be as brief as possible upon this subject, keeping in view meanwhile that candor and perspicuity which are indispensable in all our attempts to explain new views.

Mood signifies *manner*. Applied to verbs it explains *how*, in *what manner*, by what means, under what circumstances, actions are performed.

There are *three* moods, the *indicative* or declarative, the *imperative* or commanding, and the *infinitive* or unlimited.

The indicative mood declares an action to be *done* or *doing, not done*, or *not doing*. It is always in the past or present tense; as, David *killed* Goliath; scholars *learn* knowledge; I *spoke not* a word; they *sing not*.

The imperative mood denotes a command given from the first *person* to the *second, to do* or *not do* an action. It expresses the wish or desire of the first person to have a certain action performed which depends on the agency of the second. The command is *present*, but the action signified by the word is *future* to the giving of the command. The second person cannot comply with the will of the first till such will is made known; as, bring me a book; go to the door.

The *infinitive* mood has no direct personal agent, but is produced as a necessary consequence, growing out of a certain condition of things. It is always *future* to such condition; that is, some prior arrangement must be had before such consequences will follow. It is always *future*; as, they are collecting a force *to besiege* the city. We study grammar *to acquire* a knowledge of language. Windows are made *to admit* light. The act of besieging the city depends on the previous circumstance, the collection of a force *to do* it. Were there no windows, the light would not be admitted to the room.

These distinctions in regard to action must be obvious to every hearer. You all are aware of the fact that action necessarily implies an actor, as every effect must have an efficient cause; and such action clearly or distinctly *indicated*, must have such an agent to produce it. 2d. You are acquainted with the fact that one person can express his will to the second, directing him to do or avoid some thing. 3d. From an established condition of things, it is easy to deduce a consequence which will follow, in the nature of things, as an unavoidable result of such a combination of power, cause, and means.

With these principles you are all familiar, whether you have studied grammar or not. They are clearly marked, abundantly simple, and must be obvious to all. They form the only necessary, because the only real, distinction, in the formation and use of the verb to express action. Any minor distinctions are only calculated to perplex and embarrass the learner.

But some grammarians have passed these natural barriers, and built to themselves schemes to accord with their own vain fancies. The remarks of Mr. Murray upon this point are very appropos. He says:

"Some writers have given our moods a much greater extent than we have assigned to them. They assert that the english language may be said, without any great impropriety, to have as many moods as it has auxiliary verbs; and they allege, in support of their opinion, that the compound expression which they help to form, point out those various dispositions and actions, which, in other languages, are expressed by moods. This would be to multiply the moods without advantage. It is, however, certain, that the conjugation or variation of verbs, in the english language, is effected, almost entirely, by the means of auxiliaries. We must, therefore, accommodate ourselves to this circumstance; and do that by their assistance, which has been done in the learned languages (a few instances to the contrary excepted) in another manner, namely, by varying the form of the verb itself. At the same time, it is necessary to set proper bounds to this business, so as not to occasion obscurity and perplexity, when we mean to be simple and perspicuous. Instead, therefore, of making a separate mood for every auxiliary verb, and introducing moods *interrogative, optative, promissive, hortative, precative,* &c., we have exhibited such only as are obviously distinct; and which, whilst they are calculated to unfold and display the subject intelligibly to the learner, seem to be sufficient, and not more than sufficient, to answer all the purposes for which moods were introduced.

"From grammarians who form their ideas, and make their decisions, respecting this part of english grammar, on the principles and constructions of languages which, in these points, do not suit the peculiar nature of our own, but differ considerably from it, we may naturally expect grammatical schemes that are not very perspicuous nor perfectly consistent, and which will tend more to perplex than to inform the learner."

Had he followed this rule, he would have saved weeks and months to every student in grammar in the community. But his remarks were aimed at Mr. Harris, who was by far the most popular writer on language in England at that time. He has adopted the very rules of Mr. Murray, and carried them out. By a careful observance of the different forms and changes of the verb and its auxiliaries, he makes out quite evidently to his own mind, *fourteen* moods, which I forbear to name.

Most grammarians contend for *five* moods, two of which, the *potential* or powerful, and the *subjunctive,* are predicated on the same principles as Mr. Harris' optative, interrogative, etc., which they condemn. It is impossible to explain the character of these moods so as to be understood. *If,* it is said, is the sign of the subjunctive, and *may* and *can* of the potential; and yet they are often found together; as, "I will go *if I can.*" No scholar can determine in what mood to put this last verb. It of right belongs to both the potential and subjunctive. *If* I *may* be allowed to speak my mind, I *should* say that such distinctions were false.

I will not go into an exposure of these useless and false distinctions, which are adopted to help carry out erroneous principles. The only pretence for a subjunctive mood is founded on the fact that *be* and *were* were formerly used in a character different from what they are at present. *Be* was used in the indicative mood, present tense, when doubt or supposition was implied; as, If I *be* there; if they *be* wise. *Be* I a man, and *receive* such treatment? *Were* was also used instead of *was* in the past tense; as, "*Were* I an American I would fight for liberty. If I *were* to admit the fact." In this character these words are rapidly becoming obsolete. We now say, "If I *am* there; am I a man, and *receive* such abuses? *was* I an American; if I was to admit," etc.

All the round about, perplexing, and tedious affair of conjugating verbs thro the different modes and tenses will appear in its true character, when we come to give you a few brief examples, according to truth and plain sense. But before doing that it will be necessary to make some remarks on time.

Tense means *time*. We distinguish time according to certain events which are generally observed. In the use of the verb we express action in reference to periods of time when it is performed.

There are three tenses, or divisions of time; *past, present*, and *future*.

Past tense applies to actions which are accomplished; as, I *wrote* a book; he *recited* his lesson.

Present tense denotes actions commenced, but not finished, and now in operation; as, he *reads* his book; we *sit* on our seats and *hear* the lecture.

Future tense refers to actions, which are *to take* place hereafter; as, I am *to go* from the Institute; we desire *to learn* grammar correctly.

Every body can mark three plain distinctions of time, past, present, and future. With the past we have been acquainted. It has ceased to be. Its works are ended. The present is a mere line—, nothing as it were—which is constantly passing unchecked from the past to the future. It is a mere division of the past and future. The Hebrew, which is strictly a philosophic language, admits no present; only a *past* and *future*. We speak of the present as denoting an action begun and not finished. In the summer, we say the trees grow, and bear fruit. But when the fruit is fallen, and the leaves seared by the frost, we change the expression, and say, it *grew* and *bore* fruit.

Of the *future* we can know nothing definitely. Heaven has hung before all human eyes an impenetrable veil which obscures all future events. No man without prophetic vision bestowed by Him who "sees the end from the beginning," can know what is *to be*, and no expression can be made, no words employed which will positively declare a future action. We may see a present condition of things, and from it argue what is *to be*, or take place hereafter; but all that knowledge is drawn from the past and deduced from a review of the present relation and tendencies of things.

I hold the paper near the fire and you say it *will* burn, and you say truly, for it has a *will*, or what is the same, an inherent tendency *to burn*. It is made of combustible matter, like paper which we have seen burn, and hence we argue this has the same tendency to be consumed. But how does your mind arrive at that fact? If you had never seen a substance like it burn, why should you conclude this *will*? Does the child know it *will* burn? No; for it has not yet learned the quality of the paper. It is not till the child has been burned that it dreads the fire. Suppose I take some asbestus, of the kind called amianthus, which is a mineral, and is formed of slender flexible fibres like flax; and in eastern countries, especially in Savoy and Corsica, is manufactured into cloth, paper, and lamp wicks. It was used in making winding sheets for the dead, in which the bodies were burned, and the ashes, retained in the incombustible sheet, were gathered into an urn, and revered as the manes of the dead. Suppose I take some of this incombustible paper or cloth, and present to you. You say it *will* burn. Why do you say thus? Because you have seen other materials which appear like this, consume to ashes. Let us put it into the fire. It *will not* burn. It has no *tendency* to burn; no quality which will consume. But this is a new idea to you and hence your mistake. You did not know it *would* burn, nor could you *indicate* such a fact. You only told your opinion derived from the present appearance of things, and hence you made an assertion in the *indicative* mood, present tense, and added to it an *infinitive* mood, in order to deduce the consequence of this future action—it *wills*, or has a *tendency* to burn. But you were mistaken, because ignorant of the *nature* of things. This amianthus looks like flax, and to a person unacquainted with it, appears to be as truly combustible; but the mineralogist, and all who know its properties, know very well that it *will* not—wills nothing, has no inclination, or tendency, to burn.

Take another example. Here is a steel needle. I hold it before you. You say, "if I let go of it, it *will* fall," and you say correctly, for it has such a tendency. But suppose a magnet, as great as that which is said to have drawn the iron coffin of Mohammed to the roof of the temple at Mecca, should be placed in the room above us. The needle, instead of falling to the floor, would be drawn in the nearest direction to that magnet. The *will* or *tendency* of the needle, as generally understood, would be overcome, the natural law of gravitation would lose its influence, by the counteracting power of the loadstone.

I say, "I will go home in an hour." But does that expression *indicate* the act of *going*? It is placed in the indicative mood in our grammars; and *go* is the principal, and *will* the auxiliary verb. May be I shall fall and die before I reach my home. But the expression is correct; *will* is *present*, go *future*. I *will*, I now *resolve*, am now inclined *to go* home.

You see the correctness of our position, that we can not positively assert a future active in the indicative mood. Try and form to yourselves a phrase by which it can be done. Should you succeed, you would violate a law of nature. You would penetrate the dark curtain of the future, and claim to yourself what you do not possess, a power to declare future actions. Prophets, by the help of the Almighty, had this power conferred upon them. But in the revelation of the sublime truths they were instructed to make known, they were compelled to adopt human language, and make it agree with our manner of speech.

The only method by which we express a future event, is to make an assertion in the indicative mood, present tense, and to that append the natural consequence in the infinitive or unlimited; as, I *am to go* to Boston. He is preparing *to visit* New-York. The infinitive mood is always future to the circumstance on which it depends.

Mr. Murray says, that "tense, being the distinction of time, might seem to admit of only the present, past, and future; but to mark it more *accurately*, it is made to consist of six variations, viz.: the present, imperfect, perfect, pluperfect, first and second future tenses." This *more accurate mark*, only serves to expose the author's folly, and distract the learner's mind. Before, all was plain. The past, present, and future are distinct, natural divisions, easily understood by all. But what idea can a person form of an *imperfect* tense in action. If there was ever such an action in the world, it was when *grammarians* MADE their grammars, which is, if I mistake not, according to their own authority, in the *im-perfect* tense! I *wrote* a letter. He *read* his piece well. The scholar learn*ed* and recit*ed* his lesson *perfectly*; and yet *learned*, tho made *perfect* by the qualification of an *adverb*, is an *imperfect* action!

But this explains the whole mystery in the business of grammar. We can here discover the cause of all the troubles and difficulties we have encountered in the whole affair. When authors *made* their books, they *did* it *imperfectly*; when teachers *taught* them, it was *imperfectly*; and when scholars *learned* them, it was *imperfectly*!! So at last, we have found the origin of this whole difficulty, in the grammars themselves; it was all imperfectly done.

But here, again, *mirabile dictu!* wonderful to tell, we are presented with a *plu-perfect* tense; that is,—*plus* means *more*,—a *more* than perfect tense! What must that be? If a thing is perfect, we can not easily conceive any thing beyond. That is a *ne plus ultra* to all advancement—there can be no more beyond. If any change is introduced, it must be by falling from *perfect* back to *imperfect*.

I *have said*, "many of the distinctions in the grammar books *have proved* mischievous; that they are as false as frivolous;" and this is said *perfectly*, in the perfect tense. If I should say, "they *had been* of some benefit," that would be *more* than *perfect*—plu-perfect. But when I say, "they *exhibited* great depth of research, and *conveyed* some light on the subject of which they *treated*," it would all be *im*-perfect.

Next, we are presented with a *second future* tense, which attempts a division of time unbounded and unknown. In the greek, they have what is called a "*paulo post future*," which in plain english, means a "*little after the future*;" that is, I suppose, when futurity has come to an end, this tense will commence! At that time we may expect to meet a "*præter plus quam perfectum*"—a more than perfect tense! But till that period shall arrive, we see little need of making such false and unphilosophic distinctions.

A teacher once told me that he explained the distinctions of time to his scholars from the clock dial which stood in the school room. Suppose *twelve* o'clock represents the *present* tense; *nine* would signify the *perfect*; any thing between nine and twelve would be *imperfect*; any thing beyond, *pluperfect*. On the other hand, any act, forward of twelve, would be *future*; and at *three* the *second future* would commence. I remarked that I thought this a wonderful improvement, especially to those who were able to have clocks by which to teach grammar, but that I could not discover why he did not have *three future*, as well as *three past* tenses. Why, he said, there were no such tenses marked in the books, and hence there was no occasion to explain them. I asked him why he did not have a tense for every hour, and so he could distinguish with Mr. Webster, *twelve* tenses, without any trouble whatever; and, by going three times round the dial, he could easily prove the correctness of Dr. Beattie's division; for he says, in his grammar, there are *thirty-six* tenses, and thinks there can not be less without "introducing confusion in the grammatical *art*." But he thought such a course would serve rather to perplex than enlighten; and so thought I. But he was the teacher of a popular school in the city of ——, and had published a duodecimo grammar of over 300 pages, entitled "Murray's Grammar, *improved*, by ——." I will not give his name; it would be libellous!

Mr. Murray thinks because certain things which he asserts, but does not prove, are found in greek and latin, "we may doubtless apply them to the english verb; and extend the principle *as far as convenience*, and the idiom of our language require." He found it to his "convenience" to note *six* principal, and as many *indefinite* tenses. Mr. Webster does the same. Dr. Beattie found it "convenient" to have *thirty-six*. In the greek they have *nine*. Mr. Bauzee distinguishes in the french *twenty* tenses; and the royal academy of Spain present a very learned and elaborate treatise on *seven future tenses* in that language. The clock dial of my friend would be found quite "*convenient*" in aiding the "convenience" of such distinctions.

The fact is, there are only three real divisions of time in any language, because there are only three in nature, and the ideas of all nations must agree in this respect. In framing language it was found impossible to mark any other distinctions, without introducing other words than those which express simple action. These words became compounded in process of time, till they are now used as changes of the same verb. I would here enter into an examination of the formation of the tenses of greek, latin, french, spanish, and german verbs, did I conceive it necessary, and show you how, by compounding two words, they form the various tenses found in the grammars. But it will be more edifying to you to confine my remarks to our own language. Here it will be found impossible to distinguish more than three tenses, or find the verb in any different form, except by the aid of other words, wholly foreign from those that express the action under consideration.

It is by the aid of auxiliary verbs that the perfect, pluperfect, or future tenses are formed. But when it is shown you that these are principal verbs, and like many other words, are used before the infinitive mood without the word *to* prefixed to them, you will perceive the consistency of the plan we propose. That such is the fact we have abundant evidence to show, and with your consent we will introduce it in this place. I repeat, all the words long considered auxiliaries, are *principal* verbs, declarative of positive action, and as such are in extensive use in our language. We can hardly agree that the words *will, shall, may, must, can, could, would, should,* etc. have no meaning, as our grammars and dictionaries would teach us; for you may look in vain for a definition of them, as principal verbs, with a few exceptions.

The reason these words are not found in the same relation to other words, with a *to* after them, is because they are so often used that we are accustomed to drop that word. The same may be said of all small words in frequent use; as, *bid, do, dare, feel, hear, have, let, make, see,* and sometimes *needs, tell,* and a few others. Bid him go. I *dare say* so. I *feel* it *move.* We *hear* him *sing. Let* us *go. Make* him *do* it. He *must go* thro Samaria. *Tell* him *do* it immediately.

It is a singular fact, but in keeping with neuter verb systems, that all the *neuter* verbs as well as the active, take these auxiliary or *helping* verbs, which, according to their showing *help them do nothing*—"express neither action or passion." A wonderful *help* indeed!

WILL. This verb signifies to *wish*, to *resolve*, to *exercise volition*, in reference to a certain thing or action. "I will go." I *now resolve* to perform the act of going. When applied to inanimate things incapable of volition, it signifies what is analogous to it, *inherent tendency*; as, paper *will* burn; iron *will* sink; water *will* run. All these things have an inherent or active tendency to change. Water is composed of minute particles of a round form, piled together. While on a level they do not move; but let a descent be made, and these particles, under the influence of gravitation, *will* change position, and roll one over another with a rapidity equalled to the condition in which they are placed. The same may be observed in a quantity of shot opened at one side which *will* run thro the aperture; but the particles being larger, they will not find a level like water. Grain, sand, and any thing composed of small particles, *will* exhibit the same tendency. Iron, lead, or any mineral, in a state of igneous solution, *will* run, has the same *inclination* to run as water, or any other liquid. In oil, tallow, and lard, when expanded by heat, the same tendency is observed; but severely chilled with the cold, it congeals, and *will* not, has no such *tendency*, to run.

You have doubtless observed a cask filled with water and nearly tight, (if it is possible, make it quite so,) and when an aperture is made in the side, it *will* run but a trifle before it will stop. Open a vent upon the top of the cask and it *will* run freely. This *will* or tendency was counteracted by other means which I will not stop here to explain.

This is a most important word in science, physical and moral, and may be traced thro various languages where it exerts the same influence in the expression of thought.

"To avoid multiplying of words, I would crave leave here, under the word *action*, to comprehend the *forbearance* too of any action proposed; *sitting still*, or *holding one's peace*, when *walking* or *speaking* are proposed, tho mere forbearances, requiring as much the determination of the *will*, and being as often weighty in their consequences as the *contrary actions*, may, on that consideration, well enough pass for actions too. For he that shall turn his thoughts inwards upon what passes in his mind when he *wills*, shall see that the *will* or power of volition is conversant about nothing."—*Locke's Essay*, b. II. c. 21. § 30.

It is correctly applied by writers to *matter* as well as mind, as may be seen by consulting their works.

"Meanwhile as nature *wills*, night bids us rest."

Milton.

The *lupulis,* or common hop, *feels* for some elevated object which will assist it in its high aspirations, and *will* climb it by winding from left to right, and *will* not be obliged to go in an opposite direction; while the *phaseolus,* or kidney bean, takes the opposite direction. Neither *will* be compelled to change its course. They *will* have their own way, and grow as they please, or they *will* die in the contest for liberty.

Arsenic has a *tendency* in itself, a latent power, which only requires an opportunity suited to its objects, when it *will act* in the most efficacious manner. It *will* destroy the life of the Emperor, who has *voluntarily* slain his thousand and tens of thousands. This secret power does not reside in the flour of wheat, for that *will not,* has no tendency, to produce such disastrous consequences.

This word is applied in a similar manner to individuals and nations. The man *will* fall, not of intention, but of accident. He *will* kill himself. The man *will* drown, and the boat *will* swim. The water *will* hold up the boat, but it *will* allow the man to sink. The Russians *will* conquer the Turks. If conquest depended solely on the *will,* the Turks would as soon conquer as the Russians. But I have not time to pursue this topic farther. You can follow out these hints at your leisure.

SHALL signifies to be *bound, obligated,* or *required,* from external necessity. Its etymology may be traced back thro various languages. It is derived direct from the saxon *scaelan* or *scylan,* and is found as a principal verb in that language, as well as in ours. In the church homily they say, "To Him alone we *schall us* to devote ourselves;" we *bind* or *obligate* ourselves. Chaucer, an early english poet, says.

"The faith we *shall* to God."

Great difficulty has been found in distinguishing between *shall* and *will,* and frequent essays have been written, to give arbitrary rules for their use. If the words were well understood, there could be no difficulty in employing them correctly. *Will* signifies *inherent tendency, aptitude,* or *disposition*, and *volition* in beings capable of using it. *Shall* implies *external necessity*, or foreign obligation. The parent says, "You *will* suffer misery if you do evil," for it is in accordance with the nature of things for evil to produce misery. "You *shall* regard my wishes," for you are under *obligation*, from the relation in which you stand to me, to do so. Let these words be clearly explained, and there will be no difficulty in using them correctly.

MAY, past tense *might*. This verb expresses *power, strength*, or *ability* to perform an action. It is a mistake that it means permission or liberty only. It implies more than that, the delegation of a power to perform the contemplated action. Suppose the scholar should faint, would the teacher say to him you *may* go into the open air? He has no *power, might*, or *strength*, communicated by such liberty, and must receive the *might* or strength of others to carry him out. But to the scholar in health he says you *may* go out, thereby giving to him a power and liberty sufficient to perform the action. This is done on the same principle that one man gives another a "*power* of attorney" to transact his business; and that *power* constitutes his *liberty* of action.

MUST signifies to be *confined, limited, bound*, or *restrained*. I *must*, or am bound, to obey; certain obligations require me to obey. The adjective of this word is in common use. The air in the cask is *musty*. It has long been *bound* or *confined* there, and prevented from partaking of the purifying qualities of the atmosphere, and hence has become *musty*.

CAN. This word is found as a principal verb and as a noun in our language, especially in the Scotch dialect. "I *ken* nae where he'd gone." Beyond the *ken* of mortals. Far from all human *ken*. It signifies to *know*, to perceive, to understand. I knew not where he had gone. Beyond the knowledge of mortals. Far from all human reach. To *con* or *cun* is a different spelling of the same word. *Cunning* is that quick *perception* of things, which enables a person to use his knowledge adroitly. The child *can* read; *knows* how to read. It *can* walk. Here it seems to imply *power*; but power, in this case, as in most others, is gained only by knowledge, for KNOWLEDGE IS POWER. Many children have strength sufficient to walk, long before they do. The reason why they *can not* walk, is, they do not *know how*; they have not learned to balance themselves in an erect position, so as to move forward without falling.

A vast proportion of human ability is derived from knowledge. There is not a being in creation so entirely incapable of self-support, as the new-born infant; and yet, by the help of knowledge, he becomes the lord of this lower world. Bonaparte was once as helpless as any other child, and yet by dint of *can, ken, cunning,* or knowledge, he made all Europe tremble. But his knowledge was limited. He became blind to danger, bewildered by success, and he *could* no longer follow the prudent course of wisdom, but fell a sacrifice to his own unbridled ambition, and blinded folly. An enlightened people *can* govern themselves; but *power* of government is gained by a knowledge of the principles of equality, and mutual help and dependency; and whenever the people become ignorant of that fact, they *will* fall, the degraded victims of their own folly, and the wily influence of some more knowing aspirant for power.

This is a most important topic; but I dare not pursue it farther, lest I weary your patience. A few examples *must* suffice.

> "Jason, she cried, for aught I *see* or *can,*
> This deed," &c.
>
> *Chaucer.*

> A famous man,
> Of every *witte* somewhat he *can,*
> *Out take* that him lacketh rule,
> His own estate to guide and rule.
>
> *Gower.*

Do has been called a *helping* verb; but it needs little observation to discover that it is no more so than a hundred other words. "*Do* thy diligence to come before winter." "*Do* the work of an evangelist."—*Paul to Timothy.* I *do* all in my power *to expose* the error and wickedness of false teaching. *Do* afford relief. *Do* something to afford relief.

HAVE has also been reckoned as an auxiliary by the "helping verb grammars," which has no other duty to perform than help conjugate other verbs thro some of their moods and tenses. It is a word in very common use, and of course must possess a very important character, which should be carefully examined and distinctly known by all who desire a knowledge of the construction of our language.

The principal difficulty in the explanation of this word, is the peculiar meaning which some have attached to it. It has been defined to denote *possession* merely. But when we say, a man *has* much *property destroyed* by fire, we do not mean that he *gains* or *possesses* much property by the fire; nor can we make *has* auxiliary to *destroyed*, for in that case it would stand thus: a man *has destroyed* much property by fire, which would be false, for the destruction was produced by an incendiary, or some other means wholly unknown to him.

You at once perceive that *to possess* is not the only meaning which attaches to *have*. It assumes a more important rank. It can be traced, with little change in form, back thro many generations. It is the same word as *heave*, originally, and retains nearly the same meaning. Saxon *habban*, Gothic *haban*, German *haben*, Latin *habeo*, French *avoir*, are all the same word, varied in spelling more than in sound; for *b* in many languages is sounded very much like *v*, or *bv*. It may mean to *hold, possess, retain, sway, control, dispose of*, either as a direct or *relative* action; for a man sustains relations to his actors, duties, family, friends, enemies, and all the world, as well as to his possessions. He *has* a hard task to perform. He *has* much pain *to suffer*. He *has* suffered much unhappiness.

I *have written* a letter. I *have* a written letter. I *have* a letter *written*. These expressions differ very little in meaning, but the verb *have* is the same in each case. By the first expression, I signify that I have *caused* the letter to be *written*; by the second that I have a letter on which such action has been performed; and by the third, that such written letter stands in such relation to myself.

I *have written* a letter and sent it away. *Written* is the past participle from *write*; as an adjective it describes the letter in the condition I placed it; so that it will be defined, wherever it is found, as my letter; that is, some way *related* to me.

We can here account for the old *perfect tense*, which is said, "not only to refer to what is *past*, but also *to convey an allusion to the present time*." The verb is in the *present* tense, the participle is in the *past*, and hence the reason of this allusion. I *have* no *space allowed* me to go into a full investigation of this word, in its application to the expression of ideas. But it is necessary to *have* it well *understood*, as it *has* an important *service entrusted* to it; and I hope you will *have* clear *views presented* to your minds, strong enough to *have* former *errors eradicated* therefrom.

If you *have* leisure *granted*, and patience and disposition equal-*ed* to the task, you have my consent to go back and read this sentence over again. You will find it *has* in it embodied much important information in relation to the use of *have* and the perfect tense.

LECTURE XIII.

ON VERBS.

Person and number in the agent, not in the action. — Similarity of agents, actions, and objects. — Verbs made from nouns. — Irregular verbs. — Some examples. — Regular Verbs. — *Ed.* — *Ing.* — Conjugation of verbs. — To love. — To have. — To be. — The indicative mood varied. — A whole sentence may be agent or object. — Imperative mood. — Infinitive mood. — Is always future.

I have said before that action can never be known separate from the actor; that the verb applies to the agent in an *acting* condition, as that term has been defined and should be understood. Hence Person and Number can never attach to the verb, but to the agent with which, of course, the action must, in every respect, agree; as, "*I write.*" In this case the action corresponds with myself. But to say that *write* is in the "first person, singular number," would be wrong, for no such number or person belongs to the verb, but is confined to myself as the agent of the action.

The form of the verb is changed when it agrees with the second or third person singular; more on account of habit, I apprehend, than from any reason, or propriety as to a change of meaning in the word. We say, when using the regular *second* person singular, "*thou writest,*" a form rarely observed except in addresses to Deity, or on solemn occasions. In the *third* person, an *s* is added to the regular form; as, "*he writes.*" The old form, which was in general use at the time the common version of the Bible was published, was still different, ending in *eth*; as, *he thinketh, he writeth.* This style, altho considerably used in the last century, is nearly obsolete. When the verb agrees with the plural number it is usually the same as when it agrees with the first person; as, "*We write, you write, they write.*" There are few exceptions to these rules.

Some people have been very tenacious about retaining the old forms of words, and our books were long printed without alteration; but change will break thro every barrier, and book-makers must keep pace with the times, and put on the dress that is catered for them by the public taste; bearing in mind, meanwhile, that great and practical truths are more essential than the garb in which they appear. We should be more careful of our health of body and purity of morals than of the costume we put on. Many genteel coats wrap up corrupt hearts, and fine hats cover silly heads. What is the chaff to the wheat?

Even our good friends, the quakers, who have particularly labored to retain old forms—"the plain language,"—have failed in their attempt, and have substituted the *object* form of the pronoun for the *agent,* and say, "*thee thinks,*" for *thou thinkest.* Their mistake is even greater than the substitution of *you* for *thou.*

So far as language depends on the conventional regulation of those who use it, it will be constantly changing; new words will be introduced, and the spelling of old ones altered, so as to agree with modern pronounciation. We have all lived long enough to witness the truth of this remark. The only rule we can give in relation to this matter is, to follow our own judgments, aided by our best writers and speakers.

The words which express action, are in many cases very similar to the agents which produce them; and the objects which are the direct results produced by such action, do not differ very materially. I will give you a few examples.

Agent.	Verb.	Object.
Actors	Act	Actions
Breathers	Breathe	Breath
Builders	Build	Buildings
Coiners	Coin	Coins
Casters	Cast	Casts or castings
Drinkers	Drink	Drink
Dreamers	Dream	Dreams
Earners	Earn	Earnings

Fishers	Fish	Fishes
Gainers	Gain	Gain
Hewers	Hew	Hewings
Innkeepers	Keep	Inns
Light or lighters	Light or shed	Lights
Miners	Mine or dig	Mines
Pleaders	Plead or make	Pleas
Producers	Produce	Products
Raisers	Raise	Raisings or houses
Runners or racers	Run	Runs or races
Sufferers	Suffer	Sufferings
Speakers	Speak	Speeches
Thinkers	Think	Thoughts
Writers	Write	Writings
Workers	Work	Works

I give you these examples to show you the near alliance between *actors*, (,) and *actions*; or agents, *actions*, and objects. Such expressions as the above are inelegant, because they are uncommon; but for no other reason, for we, in numberless cases, employ the same word for agent and verb; as, *painters paint* buildings, and *artists* paint paintings; *bookbinders bind books*; *printers print* books, and other *prints*. A little observation will enable you to carry out these hints, and profit by them. You have observed the disposition in children, and foreigners, who are partially acquainted with our language, to make verbs out of almost every noun, which appears to us very aukward; but was it common, it would be just as correct as the verbs now used. There are very few verbs which have not a noun to correspond with them, for we make verbs, that is, we use words to express action, which are nearly allied to the agent with which such action agrees. [17] From botany we have made *botanize*; from Mr. McAdam, the inventor of a particular kind of road, *macadamize*, which means to make roads as he made them. Words are formed in this way very frequently. The word *church* is often used as a noun to express a building used for public worship; for the services performed in it; for the whole congregation; for a portion of believers associated together; for the Episcopal order, etc. It is also used as a verb. Mr. Webster defines it, "To perform with any one the office of returning thanks in the church after any signal deliverance." But the word has taken quite a different turn of late. *To church* a person, instead of receiving him into communion, as that term would seem to imply, signifies to deal with an offending member, to excommunicate, or turn him out.

But I will not pursue this point any farther. The brief hints I have thrown out, will enable you to discover how the meaning and forms of words are changed from their original application to suit the notions and improvements of after ages. A field is here presented which needs cultivation. The young should be taught to search for the etymology of words, to trace their changes and meaning as used at different times and by different people, keeping their minds constantly directed to the object signified by such verbal sign. This is the business of philosophy, under whatever name it may be taught; for grammar, rhetoric, logic, and the science of the mind, are intimately blended, and should always be taught in connexion. We have already seen that words without meaning are like shadows without realities. And persons can not employ language "correctly," or "with propriety," till they have acquainted themselves with the import of such language—the ideas of things signified by it. Let this course be adopted in the education of children, and they will not be required to spend months and years in the study of an "*art*" which they can not comprehend, for the simple reason that they can not apply it in practice. Grammar has been taught as a mere *art*, depending on arbitrary rules to be mechanically learned, rather than a science involving the soundest and plainest principles of philosophy, which are to be known only as developed in common practice among men, and in accordance with the permanent laws which govern human thought.

Verbs differ in the manner of forming their *past* tenses, and participles, or adjectives. Those ending in *ed* are called *regular*; those which take any other termination are *irregular*. There are about two hundred of the latter in our language, which differ in various ways. Some of them have the *past* tense and the past participle the same; as,

Bid	Bid	Bid
Knit	Knit	Knit
Shut	Shut	Shut

Let	Let	Let
Spread	Spread	Spread, etc.

Others have the past tense and participle alike, but different from the present; as,

Lend	Lent	Lent
Send	Sent	Sent
Bend	Bent	Bent
Wend	Went	Went
Build	Built or builded	Built
Think	Thought	Thought, etc.

Some have the present and past tense and participle different; as,

Blow	Blew	Blown
Grow	Grew	Grown
Begin	Began	Begun
See	Saw	Seen
Write	Wrote	Written
Give	Gave	Given
Speak	Spoke	Spoken
Rise	Rose	Risen
Fall	Fell	Fallen, etc.

There are a few which are made up of different radicals, which have been wedded together by habit, to avoid the frequent and unpleasant recurrence of the same word; as,

Am	Was	Been
Go (wend)	Went	Gone, etc.

Some which were formerly irregular, are now generally used with the regular termination, in either the past tense or participle, or both; as,

Hang	Hung or hanged	Hung or hanged
Dare	Dared or durst	Dared
Clothe	Clad or clothed	Clad or clothed
Work	Worked or wrought	Worked
Shine	Shined or shone	Shone or shined
Spill	Spilled or spilt	Spilt or spilled, etc.

The syllable *ed* is a contraction of the past tense of *do*; as, I *loved*, love *did*, *did* love, or love-*ed*. He learn*ed*, learn did, did learn, or learned. It signifies action, *did*, done, or accomplished. You have all lived long enough to have noticed the change in the pronounciation of this syllable. Old people sound it full and distinct; and so do most others in reading the scriptures; but not so generally as in former times. In poetry it was usually abbreviated so as to avoid the full sound; and hence we may account for the *irregular* termination of many words, such as *heard*, for *heared*; *past*, for *passed*; *learnt*, for *learned*; *built*, for *builded*. In modern poetry, however, the *e* is retained, tho sounded no more than formerly.

Ing is derived from the verb to *be*, and signifies *being, existing*; and, attached to a verb, is used as a noun, or adjective, retaining so much of its former character as to have an object after it which is affected by it; as, "I am *writing* a lecture." Here *writing*, the present participle of *write*, describes myself in my present employment, and yet retains its action as a verb, and terminates on *lecture* as the thing written. "The man was taken in the act of *stealing* some money." In this case *stealing* names the action which the man was performing when detected, which action thus named, has *money* for the object on which it terminates.

I barely allude to this subject in this place to give you an idea of the method we adopt to explain the meaning and use of participles. It deserves more attention, perhaps, to make it plain to your minds; but as it is not an essential feature in the new system, I shall leave it for consideration in a future work. Whoever is acquainted with the formation of the present participle in other languages, can carry out the suggestions I have made, and fully comprehend my meaning.

I will present you with an example of the conjugations of a few verbs which you are requested to compare with the "*might could would should have been loved*" systems, which you were required to learn in former times. You will find the verb in every *form* or position in which it ever occurs in our language, written or spoken.

Conjugation of the regular verb TO LOVE.

INDICATIVE MOOD.

	Singular	*Plural*
	I *love*	We *love*
Present tense	Thou *lovest*	You *love*
	He, she, or it *loves*	They *love*
	I *loved*	We *loved*
Past tense	Thou *lovedst*	You *loved*
	He, she, or it *loved*	They *loved*

IMPERATIVE MOOD.

Love.

INFINITIVE MOOD.

To love.

PARTICIPLES.

Present, *Loving*
Past, *Loved*

The irregular verb TO HAVE, is thus conjugated.

INDICATIVE MOOD.

I *have*	We *have*

Present tense	Thou *hast*	You *have*
	He *has*	They *have*
Past tense	I *had*	We *had*
	Thou *hadst*	You *had*
	He *had*	They *had*

IMPERATIVE MOOD.

Have.

INFINITIVE MOOD.

To have.

PARTICIPLES.

Present, *Having*
Past, *Had*

The irregular verb TO BE, stands thus:

INDICATIVE MOOD.

	I *am*	We *are*
Present tense	Thou *art*	You *are*
	He *is*	They *are*
	I *was*	We *were*
Past tense	Thou *wast*	You *were*
	He *was*	They *were*

IMPERATIVE MOOD.

Be.

INFINITIVE MOOD.

To be.

PARTICIPLES.

Present, *Being*
Past, *Been*

These examples will suffice to give you an idea of the ease and simplicity of the construction of verbs, and by a comparison with old systems, you can, for yourselves, determine the superiority of the principles we advocate. The above tabular views present every form which the verb assumes, and every position in which it is found. In use, these words are frequently compounded together;[18] but with a knowledge of the above principles, and the *meaning* of the words—a most essential consideration—you will always be able to analyze any sentence, and parse it correctly. I have not time to enlarge on this point, to show how words are connected together. Nor do I think it necessary to enable you to understand my views. To children such a work would be indispensable, and shall be attended to if we are able to publish a grammar containing the simple principles of language.

The indicative mood is varied four ways. 1st, affirmatively, *he writes*; 2d, negatively, *he writes not*; 3d, interrogatively, *does* he write? or *writes* he? 4th, suppositively, if *he writes*, *suppose he writes*, allow *he writes*.

The *first* is a simple affirmation of a fact, and is easily understood. The *second* is formed by annexing a term to express negation. *Not* is a contraction from *nought* or *naught*, which is a compound of *ne*, negative, and ought or aught, *ne-aught*, meaning *no-thing*. *He writes not*; he writes nothing. He does *not* write; he does *nothing* to write. *Neither* is a compound of *ne* and *either*, *not either*. He *can not* read; he *can, kens, knows nothing*, has no ability *to read*.

The third is constructed into a question by placing the verb before the agent, or by prefixing another word before the agent, and then placing the former verb as an infinitive after it; as, *Does* he write? or *writes* he? When another verb is prefixed, one is always chosen which will best decide the query. Does he *any thing* to write? Does he make any motions or show any indications to write? When the *will* or disposition of a person is concerned, we choose a word accordingly. *Will* he write? Has he the *will* or disposition to write? *Can* he write? Is he able—*knows* he how to write? A little observation will enable you to understand my meaning.

In the fourth place, a supposition is made in the imperative mood, in accordance with which the action is performed. "*If* ye *love* me, keep my commandments." *Give, grant, allow, suppose* this fact—you *love* me, keep my commandments. I will go if I can. I *resolve, will,* or *determine* to go; *if, gif, give,* grant, allow this fact, I *can, ken, know* how, or *am* able *to go.* But more on this point when we come to the consideration of contractions.

In this mood the verb must have an agent and object, expressed or implied; as, "*farmers* cultivate the *soil.*" But a whole sentence, that is, an idea written out, may perform this duty; as, "The study of grammar, on false principles, is productive of no good." What is productive of no good? What is the agent of *is*? "The *study,*" our books and teachers tell us. But does such a construction give the true meaning of the sentence? I think not, for *study* is indispensable to knowledge and usefulness, and *the study* of grammar, properly directed, is a most useful branch of literature, which should never be dispensed with. It is the study of grammar *on false principles,* which *is productive of no good.* You discover my meaning, and will not question its correctness. You must also see how erroneous it would be to teach children that "*to study* is productive of no good." The force of the sentence rests on the "false principles" taught. Hence the whole statement is truly the agent of the verb.

The object on which the action terminates is frequently expressed in a similar manner; as, "He wrote to me, that he will adopt the new system of grammar, if he can procure some books to give his scholars to learn." Will you parse *wrote*? Most grammarians will call it an *intransitive* verb, and make out that "he wrote" *nothing* to me, because there is no regular objective word after it. Will you parse *that*? It is a "conjunction *copulative.*" What does it connect? "*He wrote*" to the following sentence, according to Rule 18 of Mr. Murray; "conjunctions connect the *same* moods and tenses of verbs and cases of nouns and pronouns." Unluckily you have two different tenses connected in this case. Will you parse *if*? It is a *copulative* conjunction, connecting the two members of the sentence—*he will adopt* if *he can procure*: Rule, as above. How exceeding unfortunate! You have *two* different moods, and too different tenses, connected by a *copulative* conjunction which the rule says "connects *the same* moods and tenses! What nonsense! What a falsehood! What a fine thing to be a grammarian! And yet, I venture the opinion, and I judge from what I have seen in myself and others, there is not one teacher in a hundred who will not learn children to parse as above, and apply the same rule to it. "I *will go* if I *can*." "I *do* and *will* contend." "As it *was* in the beginning, *is* now, *and* ever *shall be*." "I *am* here and *must* remain." "He *will do* your business *if* he *has* time." "I *am* resolved *to expose* the errors of grammar, *and will do* it thoroly *if* I *can*."

In these examples you have different moods and tenses, indiscriminately, yet correctly coupled together, despite the rules of syntax which teach us to explain language "with propriety."

That, in the sentence before us, is an adjective, referring to the following sentence, which is the *object* of *wrote*, or is the thing written. "He wrote to me *that*" fact, sentiment, opinion, determination, or resolution, that writing, letter, or word—"he will adopt the new system of grammar, if he can procure some books."

This subject properly belongs to that department of language called syntax; but as I shall not be able to treat of that in this course of lectures, I throw in here these brief remarks to give you some general ideas of the arrangement of words into sentences, according to their true meaning, as obtained from a knowledge of their etymology. You cannot fail to observe this method of constructing language if you will pay a little attention to it when reading; keeping all the time in view the fact that words are only the signs of ideas, derived from an observation of things. You all know that it is not merely the steam that propels the boat, but that it is steam *applied to machinery*. Steam is the more latent cause; and the engine with its complicated parts is the direct means. In the absence of either, the boat would not be propelled. In the formation of language, I may say correctly, "Solomon *built* the temple;" for he stood in that relation to the matter which supposes it would not have been built without his direction and command. To accomplish such an action, however, he need not raise a hammer or a gavel, or draw a line on the trestle board. His command made known to his ministers was sufficient to *cause* the work to be done. Hence the whole fact is *indicated* or declared by the single expression, "Solomon *built* the temple."

The Imperative mood is unchanged in form. I can say to one man, *go*, or to a thousand, *go*. The commander when drilling *one* soldier, says, *march*; and he bids the whole battalion, *march*. The agent who is *to perform* the action is understood when not expressed; as, *go, go thou*, or *go you*. The agent is generally omitted, because the address is given direct to the person who is expected to obey the instruction, request, or command. This verb always agrees with an agent in the *second* person. And yet our "grammars made easy" have given us *three persons* in this mood—"*Let me love; love, love thou*, or *do* thou *love*; let him love." In the name of common sense, I ask, what can children learn by such instruction? "*Let me love*," in the conjugation of the verb *to love*! To whom is this command given? To *myself* of course! I command myself to "*let me love*!" What nonsense! "Let *him* love." I stand here, you set there, and the *third* person is in Philadelphia. I utter these words, "Let *him love*." What is my meaning? Why, our books tell us, that the verb to *love* is *third* person. Then I command *him* to *let himself love*! What jargon and falsehood! You all know that we can address the *second* person only. You would call me insane if I should employ language according to the rules of grammar as laid down in the standard books. In my room alone, no person near me, I cry out, "*let me be quiet*"—imperative mood, first person of *to be*! Do I command myself to *let* myself *be* quiet? Most certainly, if *be* is the principal verb in the first person, and *let* the auxiliary. The teacher observes one of his pupils take a pencil from a classmate who sets near him. He says, "*let him have it*." To whom is the command given? It is the imperative mood, third person of the verb *to have*. Does he command the third person, the boy who *has* not the pencil? Such is the resolution of the sentence, according to the authority of standard grammars. But where is there a child five years old who does not know better. Every body knows that he addresses the second person, the boy who has the pencil, to *let* the other *have* it.

Teachers have learned their scholars the *first* and *third* persons of this mood when committing the conjugation of verbs; but not one in ten thousand ever adopted them in parsing. "*Let me love*." *Let*, all parse, Mr. Murray not excepted, in the *second* person, and *love* in the infinitive mood after it, without the sign *to*; according to the rule, that "verbs which follow *bid, dare, feel, hear, let, needs, speak*," etc. are in the infinitive mood. It is strange people will not eat their own cooking.

There can be no trouble in understanding this mood, as we have explained it, always in the future tense, that is, future to the command or request, agreeing with the *second* person, and never varied on account of number.

The only variation in the infinitive mood is the omission of *to* in certain cases, which is considered as a part of the verb; tho in truth it is no more so than when used in the character of an old fashioned preposition. In certain cases, as we have before observed, it is not expressed. This is when the infinitive verb follows small words in frequent use; as, shall, will, let, can, must, may, bid, do, have, make, feel, hear, etc.

This mood is always in the future tense; that is, it is future to the circumstances or condition of things upon which it depends; as, they are making preparations *to raise* the building. Here *to raise* is future to the preparations, for if they make no preparations, the buildings will not be raised. The boy studies his book *to learn* his lesson. If he does not study, he will not be likely *to learn* his lesson.

The allied powers of Europe combined their forces *to defeat* Napoleon. In this instance the whole expression is in the past tense; nevertheless, the action expressed in the infinitive mood, *was future* to the circumstance on which it depended; that is, the *defeat* was *future* to the *combination* of the forces. Abraham raised the knife *to slay* his son. Not that he did *slay* him, as that sentence must be explained on the common systems, which teach us that *to slay* is in the *present tense*; but he raised the fatal knife for that purpose, the fulfilment of which was future; but the angel staid his hand, and averted the blow. The patriots of Poland *made* a noble attempt *to gain* their liberty. But they did not *gain it*, as our grammars would teach us. *To gain* was future to the attempt, and failed because the circumstances *indicated* by the event, were insufficient to produce so favorable a result.

No person of common discernment can fail to observe the absolute falsehood of existing systems in respect to this mood. It is used by our authors of grammar in the *present* and *past* tenses, but never in the *future*. Let us give a moment to the consideration of this matter. Take the following example. He *will prepare* himself next week *to go* to Europe. Let the school master parse *will prepare*. It is a verb, indicative mood, *first future* tense. *Next week* is the point in futurity when the *preparation* will be *made*. Now parse *to go*. It is a verb, infinitive mood, *present tense*! Then *he* is already on his way to Europe, when he is not *to prepare* himself till next week! An army is collected *to fight* the enemy. Is the fight already commenced? *To fight* is present tense, say the books. We shall study grammar next year, *to obtain* a knowledge of the principles and use of language. Is *to obtain* present tense? If so there is little need of spending time and money to study for a knowledge we *already possess*.

"Hope springs eternal in the human breast;
Man never *is*, but always TO BE blest."

Pope.

"Who *was*, and who *is*, and who *is* TO COME."—*Bible.* It is not that a man thinks himself already in possession of a sufficiency, but hopes TO BE qualified, etc.

I *am to go* in an hour. He *is to go* to-morrow. I *am* ready *to hear* you recite your lesson. He *has been waiting* a long time *to see* if some new principles will not be introduced. He is prepared *to appear* before you whenever you shall direct. We *are* resolved *to employ* neuter verbs, potential and subjunctive moods, im-perfect, plu-perfect, and second future tenses, no longer. False grammars *are* only fit-*ted to be* laid aside. We are in duty bound *to regard* and *adopt* truth, and *reject* error; and we *are* determined *to do* it in grammar, and every thing else.

We are not surprised that people cannot comprehend grammar, as usually taught, for it is exceedingly difficult to make error appear like truth, or false teaching like sound sentiment. But I will not stop to moralize. The hints I have given must suffice.

Much more might be said upon the character and use of verbs; but as these lectures are not designed for *a system* of grammar *to be taught*, but to expose the errors of existing systems, and prepare the way for a more rational and consistent exposition of language, I shall leave this department of our subject, presuming you will be able to comprehend our views, and appreciate their importance. We have been somewhat critical in a part of our remarks, and more brief than we should have been, had we not found that we were claiming too much of the time of the Institute, which is designed as a means of improvement on general subjects. Enough has been said, I am sure, to convince you, if you were not convinced before, why the study of grammar is so intricate and tedious, that it is to be accounted for from the fact that the theories by which it is taught are false in principle, and can not be adopted in practice; and that something ought to be done to make the study of language easy, interesting, and practical. Such a work is here attempted; but it remains with the public to say whether these plain philosophical principles shall be sustained, matured, perfected, and adopted in schools, or the old roundabout course of useless and ineffectual teaching be still preserved.

LECTURE XIV.

ON CONTRACTIONS.

A temporary expedient. — Words not understood. — All words must have a meaning. — Their formation. — Changes of meaning and form. — Should be observed. — ADVERBS. — Ending in *ly*. — Examples. — Ago. — Astray. — Awake. — Asleep. — Then, when. — There, where, here. — While, till. — Whether, together. — Ever, never, whenever, etc. — Oft. — Hence. — Perhaps. — Not. — Or. — Nor. — Than. — As. — So. — Distinctions false. — Rule 18. — If. — But. — Tho. — Yet.

We have concluded our remarks on the necessary divisions of words. Things *named, defined* and *described*, and their *actions, relations,* and *tendencies*, have been considered under the classes of Nouns, Adjectives, and Verbs. To these classes all words belong when properly explained; a fact we desire you to bear constantly in mind in all your attempts to understand and employ language. But there are many words in our language as well as most others, which are so altered and disguised that their meaning is not easily comprehended. Of course they are difficult of explanation. These words we have classed under the head of *Contractions*, a term better calculated than any other we have seen adopted to express their character. We do not however lay any stress on the appropriateness of this appellation, but adopt it as a temporary expedient, till these words shall be better understood. They will then be ranked in their proper places among the classes already noticed.

Under this head may be considered the words usually known as "adverbs, conjunctions, prepositions, and interjections." That the etymology and meaning of these words have not been generally understood will be conceded, I presume, on all hands. In our opinion, that is the only reason why they have been considered under these different heads, for in numberless cases there is nothing in their import to correspond with such distinctions. Why "an adverb expresses some *quality* or circumstance respecting a verb, adjective, or other adverb;" why "a conjunction is chiefly used to connect sentences, so as out of *two* to make only *one* sentence;" or why "prepositions serve to connect words with one another, and show the relation between them," has never been explained. They have been *passed over* with little difficulty by teachers, having been furnished with lists of words in each "part of speech," which they require their pupils to commit to memory, and "for ever after hold their peace" concerning them. But that these words have been defined or explained in a way to be understood will not be pretended. In justification of such ignorance, it is contended that such explanation is not essential to their proper and elegant use. If such is the fact, we may easily account for the incorrect use of language, and exonerate children from the labor of studying etymology.

But these words have meaning, and sustain a most important rank in the expression of ideas. They are, generally, abbreviated, compounded, and so disguised that their origin and formation are not generally known. Horne Tooke calls them "the *wheels* of language, the *wings* of Mercury." He says "tho we might be dragged along without them, it would be with much difficulty, very heavily and tediously." But when he undertakes to show that they were *constructed* for this object, he mistakes their true character; for they were not invented for that purpose, but were originally employed as nouns or verbs, from which they have been corrupted by use. And he seems to admit this fact when he says,[19] "*abbreviation* and *corruption* are always busiest with the words which are most frequently in use. Letters, like soldiers, being very apt to desert and drop off in a long march, and especially if their passage happens to lie near the confines of an enemy's country."

In the original construction of language a set of literary men did not get together and manufacture a lot of words, finished thro out and exactly adapted to the expression of thought. Had that been the case, language would doubtless have appeared in a much more regular, stiff, and formal dress, and been deprived of many of its beautiful and lofty figures, its richest and boldest expressions. Necessity is the mother of invention. It was not until people had *ideas* to communicate, that they sought a medium for the transmission of thought from one to another; and then such sounds and signs were adopted as would best answer their purpose. But language was not then framed like a cotton mill, every part completed before it was set in operation. Single expressions, *sign*-ificant of things, or *ideas* of *things* and *actions*, were first employed, in the most simple, plain, and easy manner.[20] As the human mind advanced in knowledge, by observing the character, relations, and differences of things, words were changed, altered, compounded, and contracted, so as to keep pace with such advancement; just as many simple parts of a machine, operating on perfect and distinct principles, may be combined together and form a most complicated, curious, and powerful engine, of astonishing power, and great utility. In the adaptation of steam to locomotives, the principles on which stationary engines operated were somewhat modified. Some wheels, shafts, bands, screws, etc., were omitted, others of a different kind were added, till the whole appeared in a new character, and the engine, before fixed to a spot, was seen traversing the road with immense rapidity. The principles of the former engine, so far from being unessential, were indispensable to the construction of the new one, and should be clearly understood by him who would build or *use* the latter. So, in the formation of language, simple *first* principles must be observed and traced thro all their ramifications, by those who would obtain a clear and thoro knowledge of it, or "read and write it with propriety."

In mathematics, the four simple rules, addition, subtraction, multiplication, and division, form the basis on which that interesting science depends. The modifications of these rules, according to their various capabilities, will give a complete knowledge of all that can be known of numbers, relations, and proportions, an acme to which all may aspire, tho none have yet attained it. The principles of language are equally simple, and, if correctly explained, may be as well understood. But the difficulty under which we labor in this department of science, is the paucity of *means* to trace back to their original form and meaning many words and phrases in common use among us. Language has been employed as the vehicle of thought, for six thousand years, and in that long space has undergone many and strange modifications. At the dispersion from Babel, and the "confusion of tongues" occasioned thereby, people were thrown upon their own resources, and left to pick up by piecemeal such shreds as should afterwards be wove into a system, and adopted by their respective nations. Wars, pestilence, and famine, as well as commerce, enterprize, literature, and religion, brought the different nations into intercourse with each other; and changes were thus produced in the languages of such people. Whoever will take the trouble to compare the idioms of speech adopted by those nations whose affairs, civil, political, and religious, are most intimately allied, will be convinced of the correctness of the sentiment now advanced.

In the lapse of ages, words would not only change their form, but in a measure their meaning, so as to correspond with the ideas of those who use them. Some would become obsolete, and others be adopted in their stead. Many words are found in the Bible which are not in common use; and the manner of spelling, as well as some entire words, have been changed in that book, since it was translated and first published in 1610. With these examples you are familiar, and I shall be spared the necessity of quoting them. I have already made some extracts from old writers, and may have occasion to do so again before I close this lecture.

The words which we class under the head of Contractions, are so altered and disguised in their appearance, that their etymology and connexion are not generally understood. It may appear like pedantry in me to attempt an investigation into their origin and meaning. But to avoid that charge, I will frankly acknowledge the truth, and own my inability to do justice to this subject, by offering a full explanation of all the words which belong to this class. I will be candid, if I am not successful. But I think most of the words long considered difficult, may be easily explained; enough to convince you of the feasibility of the ground we have assumed, and furnish a sample by which to pursue the subject in all our future inquiries into the etymology of words.

But even if I fail in this matter, I shall have one comfort left, that I am not alone in the transgression; for no philologist, with few exceptions, has done any thing like justice to this subject. Our common grammars have not even attempted an inquiry into the *meaning* of these words, but have treated them as tho they had none. Classes, like pens or reservoirs, are made for them, into which they are thrown, and allowed to rest, only to be named, without being disturbed. Sometimes, however, they are found in one enclosure, sometimes in another, more by mistake, I apprehend, than by intention; for "prepositions" under certain circumstances are parsed as "adverbs," and "adverbs" as "adjectives," and "conjunctions" as either "adverbs" or "prepositions;" and not unfrequently the whole go off together, like the tail of the dragon, drawing other respectable words along with them, under the sweeping cognomen of "adverbial phrases," or "conjunctive expressions;" as, Can you write your lesson? *Not yet quite well enough.* "*But and if* that evil servant,"[21] etc. Mr. Murray says, "the same word is occasionally used *both as* a conjunction *and as* an adverb, and sometimes *as* a preposition.

Let these words be correctly defined, their meaning be ferreted out from the rubbish in which they have been enclosed; or have their dismembered parts restored to them, they will then appear in their true character, and their connexion with other words will be found regular and easy. Until such work is accomplished, they may as well be called contractions, for such they *mostly* are, as adverbs or any thing else; for that appellation we regard as more appropriate than any other.

In the attempts we are about to make, we shall endeavor to be guided by sound philosophic principles and the light of patient investigation; and whatever advances we may make shall be in strict accordance with the true and practical use of these words.

Let us begin with *Adverbs.*

I have not time to go into a thoro investigation of the mistakes into which grammarians have fallen in their attempts to explain this "part of speech." Mr. Murray says they "seem originally to have been *contrived* to express compendiously in *one word*, what must *otherwise* have required two or more; as, "he acted *wisely*." They could have been "*contrived*" for no such purpose, for we have already seen that they are made up of various words combined together, which are used to express relation, to define or describe other things. Take the very example Mr. M. has given. *Wisely* is made up of two words; *wise* and *like*. "He acted wisely," wise-like. What did he *act*? *Wisely*, we are taught, expresses the "*manner* or quality" of the verb *act*. But *act*, in this case, is a neuter or intransitive verb, and *wisely* expresses the *manner of action* where there is none! But he must have *acted something* which was *wise* like something else. What did he act? If he produced no *actions*, how can it be known that he *acted* wisely or unwisely? *Action* or *acts* is the direct object of to *act*. Hence the sentence fully stated would stand thus: "He acted *acts* or *actions* like wise actions or acts." But stated at length, it appears aukward and clumsy, like old fashioned vehicles. We have modified, improved, cut down, and made eliptical, all of our expressions, as we have previously observed, to suit the fashions and customs of the age in which we live; the same as tailors cut our garments to correspond with the latest fashions.

"The bird sings *sweetly*." The bird sings *songs, notes,* or *tunes, like sweet notes, tunes,* or *songs*. The comparison here made, is not in reference to the agent or action, but the *object* of the action; and this explains the whole theory of those *adverbs,* which are said to "qualify manner" of action. We have already seen that no *action,* as such, can exist, or be conceived to exist, separate(-ed) from the *thing* or *agent* which *acts*; and such action can only be determined by the *changed* or altered condition of something which is the *object* of such action. How then, can any word, in truth, or in thought, be known to *qualify* the action, as distinct from the object or agent? And if it does not in *fact,* how can we explain words to children, or to our own minds, so as to understand what is not true?

Hence all words of this character are adjectives, describing one thing by its relation or likeness to another, and as such, admit of comparison; as, a likely man, a *very* likely man, a likelier, and the *likeliest* man. "He is the *most likely* pedlar I ever knew." "He is *more liable* to be deceived." "A *lively* little fellow." "He is worthless." He is worth less, *less worthy* of respect and confidence. "He writes very correctly." He writes his letters and words *like very correct* letters. But I need not enlarge. You have only to bear in mind the fact, that *ly* is a contraction of *like,* which is often retained in many words; as god*like,* christian*like,* etc., and search for a definition accordingly; and you will find no trouble in disposing of a large portion of this adverb family.

It is a curious fact, and should be maturely considered by all who still adhere to the neuter verb theory, that adverbs *qualify neuter* as well as active verbs, and express the *quality* or *manner of action,* where there is none! Adverbs express "manner of action" in a neuter verb! When a person starts wrong it is very difficult to go right. The safest course is to return back and start again.

Adverbs have been divided into classes, varying from *eleven* to *seventy-two,* to suit the fancies of those who have only observed the nice shades of form which these words have assumed. But a bonnet is a bonnet, let its shape, form, or fashion, be what it may. You may put on as many trimmings, flowers, bows, and ribbons, as you please; it is a bonnet still; and when we speak of it we will call it a *bonnet,* and talk about its *appendages.* But when it is constructed into something else, then we will give it a new name.

Adjectives, we have said, are *derived* from either nouns or verbs, and we now contend that the words formerly regarded as adverbs are either adjectives, nouns, or verbs. In defence of this sentiment we will adduce a few words in this place for examples.

Ago. "Three years *ago,* we dwelt in the country." This word is a past participle from the verb *ago,* meaning the same as *gone* or *agone,* and was so used a few centuries *ago*—*agone,* or *gone by*.

"For euer the latter ende of ioye is wo,
God wotte, worldly ioye is soone *ago*."
Chaucer.

"For if it erst was well, tho was it bet
A thousand folde, this nedeth it not require
Ago was euery sorowe and euery fere."
Troylus, boke 3, p. 2.

"Of such examples as I finde
Upon this point of tyme *agone*
I thinke for to tellen one."
Gower, lib. 5, p. 1.

"Which is no more than has been done
By knights for ladies, long *agone*."
Hudibras.

"Twenty years *agone*."

Tillotson's sermon.

"Are all *the go*."

Knickerbocker.

ASTRAY. "They went astray." *Astrayed*, wandered or were scattered, and of course soon became *estranged* from each other. Farmers all know what it is for cattle to *stray* from home; and many parents have felt the keen pangs of sorrow when their sons *strayed* from the paths of virtue. In that condition they are *astray-ed*.

"This prest was drank and goth *astrayede*."

"Achab to the bottle went.
When Benedad for all his shelde
Him slough, so that upon the felde
His people goth aboute *astraie*."

Gower.

AWAKE. "He is *awake*." "Samson *awaked* out of his sleep." "That I may *awake* him out of sleep." "It is high time to *awake*." "As a man that is *wakened* out of sleep." The Irish hold *a wake*—they do not sleep the night after the loss of friends.

ASLEEP.

"When that pyte, which longe *on sleep* doth tary
Hath set the fyne of al my heuynesse."

Chaucer, La belle dame, p. 1. c. 1.

"Ful sound *on sleep* did caucht thare rest be kind."

Douglas, b. 9, p. 283.

"In these provynces the fayth of Chryste was all quenchyd and *in sleepe*."—*Fabian.*

A numerous portion of these contractions are nouns, which, from their frequent recurrence, are used without their usual connexion with small words. The letter *a* is compounded with many of these words, which may have been joined to them by habit, or as a preposition, meaning *on, to, at, in*, as it is used in the french and some other languages. You often hear expressions like these, "he is *a*-going; he is *a*-writing; he began *a*-new," etc. The old adverbs which take this letter, you can easily analyze; as, "The house is *a*-fire"—on fire; "He fell *a*-sleep"—he fell *on* sleep. "When deep sleep falleth on men."—*Job.* "He stept *a*-side"—on one side. "He came *a*-board"—on board. "They put it *a*-foot"—on foot. "He went *a*-way"—a way, followed some *course*, to a distance. "Blue bonnets are all the *go* now *a*-days," etc.

The following extracts will give you an idea of the etymology of these words:

> "Turnus seyes the Troianis in grete yre,
> And al thare schyppis and navy set *in fire*."
>
> *Douglas*, b. 9, p. 274.

> "Now hand in hand the dynt lichtis with *ane* swak,
> Now bendis he up his bourdon with *ane* mynt,
> *On side* (a-side) he bradis for to eschew the dynt."
>
> *Idem.*

> "That easter fire and flame aboute
> Both at mouth and at nase
> So that thei setten all *on blaze*," (ablaze.)
>
> *Gower.*

> "And tyl a wicked deth him take
> *Him had* leuer *asondre* (a-sunder) shake
> And let al his lymmes *asondre* ryue
> Thane leaue his richesse in his lyue."
>
> *Chaucer.*

Examples of this kind might be multiplied to an indefinite length. But the above will suffice to give you an idea of the former use of these words, and also, by comparison with the present, of the changes which have taken place in the method of spelling within a few centuries.

A large portion of adverbs relate to *time* and *place*, because many of our ideas, and much of our language, are employed in reference to them; as, *then, when, where, there, here, hence, whence, thence, while, till, whether,* etc. These are compound words considerably disguised in their meaning and formation. Let us briefly notice some of them.

Per annum is a latin phrase, *for the year*, a *year*; and *the annum* is *the year*, *round* or *period* of time, from which it was corrupted gradually into its present shape. *Thanne,* tha anne, *thane, thenne, then, than,* are different forms of the same word.

"We see nowe bi a mirror in darcnesse: thanne forsathe, face to face. Nowe I know of partye; *thanne* forsathe schal know as I am knowen."—1. Cor. 13: 12. *Translation in 1350.*

I have a translation of the same passage in 1586, which stands thus: "For nowe we see through a glasse darkley: but *thene* face to face: now I know in part: but *then* shal I know even as I am knowen." Here several words are spelled differently in the same verse.

THEN, *the anne*, that time. WHEN, *wha anne*, "*wha-icht-anne*," which, or what *anne*, period of time.

Area means an open space, a plat of ground, a spot or place. Arena is from the same etymon, altered in application. THERE, *the area*, the *place* or *spot*. "If we go *there*," to that place. WHERE, which, or what ("wha-icht area") place. HERE, *his* (latin word for *this*,) *area*, this place. These words refer to *place, state*, or *condition*.

While is another spelling for *wheel*. "To while away our time," is to *pass*, spend, or *wheel* it away. *While* applies to the *period*, or space of time, in which something *wheels, whirls, turns* round, or transpires; as, "You had better remain here *while* (during the time) he examines whether it is prudent for you to go."

Till is *to while,* to the *period* at which something is expected to follow. "If I will that he tarry *till* (to the time) I come what is that to thee?"

The idea of *time* and *place* are often blended together. It is not uncommon to hear lads and professed scholars, in some parts of our country say "down *till* the bottom, over *till* the woods." etc. Altho we do not regard such expressions correct, yet they serve to explain the meaning of the word. The only mistake is in applying it to *place* instead of *time.*

Whether is *which either.* "Shew *whether* of these *two* thou hast chosen."— *Acts 1: 24.* It is more frequently applied in modern times to circumstance and events *than to* persons and things. "I will let you know *whether* I *will* or *will not* adopt it," one or the other.

Together signifies two or more united. *Gethered* is the past participle of *gather.*

> "As Mailie, an' her lambs *thegither,*
> Were ae day nibbling on the tether."
>
> *Burns.*

Ever means *time, age, period.* It originally and essentially signified *life.* For *ever* is for the age or period. *For ever* and *ever,* to the ages of ages. *Ever-lasting* is *age-lasting.* Ever-lasting hills, snows, landmarks, etc.

Never, *ne-ever, not ever,* at no time, age or period.

When-ever.—At what point or space of *time* or *age.*

What-ever.—What thing, fact, circumstance, or event.

Where-ever.—To, at, or in what place, period, age, or time.

Whither-so-ever, which-way-so-ever, where-so-ever, never-the-less, etc. need only be analyzed, and their meaning will appear obvious to all.

Oft, *often, oft-times,* often-*times,* can be understood by all, because the noun to which they belong is *oft-en* retained in practice.

Once, twice, at one time, two times.

HENCE, *thence, whence*, from *this, that,* or *what,* place, spot, circumstance, post, or starting place.

HENCE-FOR-WARD, *hence-forth*, in time *to come*, after this period.

HERE-AFTER, after this *era*, or present time.

HITHER, to this spot or place. *Thither*, to that place. *Hither-to, hither-ward*, etc. the same as *to you ward*, or to God ward, still retained in our bibles.

PER-HAPS, it may hap. *Perchance, peradventure*, by chance, by adventure. The latin *per* means *by*.

NOT, no ought, not any, nothing. It is a compound of *ne* and *ought* or *aught*.

OR is a contraction from other, and *nor* from *ne-or*, no-or, no other.

NO-WISE, no ways. I will go, or, other-wise, in another way or manner, you must go.

THAN, *the ane*, the one, that one, alluding to a particular object with which a comparison is made; as, This book is larger *than* that bible. That *one* bible, this book is larger. It is always used with the comparative degree, to define particularly the object with which the comparison is made. Talent is better than flattery. Than flattery, often bestowed regardless of merit, talent is better.

As is an adjective, in extensive use. It means the, this, that, these, the same, etc. It is a defining word of the first kind. You practice *as* you have been taught—*the same duties* or *principles* understood. We use language *as* we have learned it; in *the same* way or manner. It is often associated with other words to particularly specify the way, manner, or degree, in which something is done or compared. I can go *as well as* you. In *the same well*, easy, convenient way or manner you can go, I can go in *the same* way. He was *as* learned, *as* pious, *as* benevolent, *as* brave, *as* faithful, *as* ardent. These are purely adjectives, used to denote the degree of the likeness or similarity between the things compared. Secondary words are often added to this, to aid the distinction or definition; as, (*the same* illustrated,) He is *just as willing*. I am *quite as well* pleased without it. *As*, like many other adjectives, often occurs without a noun expressed, in which case it was formerly parsed by Murray himself *as* (like, or the same) a relative pronoun; as, "And indeed it seldom at any period extends to the tip, *as happens* in acute diseases."—*Dr. Sweetster.* "The ground I have assumed is tenable, *as will appear.*"—*Webster.* "Bonaparte had a special motive in decorating Paris, for 'Paris is France, *as has* often been observed."—*Channing.* "The words are such *as seem.*"—*Murray's Reader! p. 16, intro.*

So has nearly the same signification as the word last noticed, and is frequently used along with it, to define the other member of the comparison. *As* far *as* I can understand, *so* far I approve. *As* he directed, *so* I obeyed. It very often occurs as a secondary adjective; as, "In pious and benevolent offices *so* simple, *so* minute, *so* steady, *so* habitual, that they will carry," etc. "He pursued a course *so* unvarying."—*Channing.*

These words are the most important of any small ones in our vocabulary, because (*for this cause*, be this the cause, this is the cause) they are the most frequently used; and yet there are no words *so* little understood, or *so* much abused by grammarians, *as* these are.

We have barely time to notice the remaining parts of speech. "Conjunctions" are defined to be a "part of speech void of signification, but so formed as to help signification, by making two or more significant sentences to be one significant sentence." Mr. Harris gives about forty "species." Murray admits of only the *dis*-junctive and copulative, and reduces the whole list of words to twenty-four. But what is meant by a *dis*-junctive *con*-junctive word, is left for you to determine. It must be in keeping with *in*definite *defining* articles, and *post*-positive *pre*-positions. He says, "it joins words, but disjoins the sense."[22] And what is a *word* with out *sense*," pray tell us? If "words are the signs of ideas," how, in the name of reason, can you give the sign and separate the sense? You can as well separate the shadow from the substance, or a quality from matter.

We have already noticed Rule 18, which teaches the use of conjunctions. Under that rule, you may examine these examples. "As it *was* in the beginning, *is* now, *and* ever *shall be*."—*Common Prayer.* "What I *do, have done,* or *may* hereafter *do, has been,* and *will* always *be* matter of inclination, the gratifying of which *pays* itself: and I *have* no more merit in employing my time and money in the way I *am known* to do, than another has in other occupations."—*Howard*.

The following examples must suffice.

IF. This word is derived from the saxon *gifan*, and was formerly written *giff, gyff, gif, geve, give, yiff, yef, yeve*. It signifies *give, grant, allow, suppose, admit*, and is always a verb in the imperative mood, having the following sentence or idea for its object. "*If* a pound of sugar cost ten cents, what will ten pounds cost?" *Give*, grant, allow, suppose, (the fact,) *one pound cost*, etc. In this case the supposition which stands as a predicate—*one pound of sugar cost ten cents*, is the object of *if*—the thing to be allowed, supposed, or granted, and from which the conclusion as to the cost of *ten* pounds is to be drawn.

"He will assist us if he has the means." Allow, admit, (the fact,) he has the means, he will assist us.

> "*Gif* luf be vertew, than is it leful thing;
> *Gif* it be vice, it is your undoing."
>> *Douglas* p. 95.

> "Ne I ne wol non reherce, *yef* that I may."
>> *Chaucer.*

> "She was so charitable and so pytous
> She wolde wepe *yf that* she sawe a mous
> Caught in a trappe, *if* it were deed or bledde."
>> *Prioresse.*

> "O haste and come to my master dear."

> "*Gin* ye be Barbara Allen."
>> *Burns.*

BUT. This word has two opposite significations. It is derived from two different radicals. *But*, from the saxon *be* and *utan, out*, means *be out, leave out, save, except, omit,* as, "all *but* one are here." *Leave out, except, one,* all are here.

> "Heaven from all creation hides the book of fate
> All *but* (*save, except*) the page prescribed our present state."

> "When nought *but* (*leave out*) the *torrent* is heard on the hill,
> And nought *but* (*save*) the nightingale's *song* in the grove."

"Nothing *but fear* restrains him." In these cases the direct *objects* of the verb, the things to be omitted are expressed.

But is also derived from *botan,* which signifies *to add, superadd, join* or *unite*; as, in the old form of a deed, "it is *butted* and bounded as follows." Two animals *butt* their heads together. The *butt* of a log is that end which was *joined* to the stump. A *butt, butment* or *a-butment* is the joined end, where there is a connexion with something else. A *butt* of ridicule is an object to which ridicule is attached.

> "Not only saw he all that was,
> But (*add*) *much* that never came to pass."
> *M'Fingal.*

To button, butt-on, is derived from the same word, to join one side to the other, to fasten together. It was formerly spelled *botan, boote, bote, bot, butte, bute, but.* It is still spelled *boot* in certain cases as a verb; as,

> "What *boots it* thee to fly from pole to pole,
> Hang o'er the earth, and with the planets roll?
> What boots ( ) thro space's fartherest bourns to roam,
> *If* thou, O man, a stranger art at home?"
> *Grainger.*

> "If love had *booted* care or cost."

A man exchanged his house in the city for a farm, and received fifty dollars to *boot*; *to add* to his property, and make the exchange equal.

Let presents the same construction in form and meaning as *but*, for it is derived from two radicals of opposite significations. It means sometimes to *permit* or *allow*; as, *let* me go; *let* me have it; and to *hinder* or *prevent*; as, "I proposed to come unto you, *but* (add this fact) I was *let* hitherto."—*Rom. 1: 13*. "He who now *letteth*, will *let* until he be taken out of the way."—*2 Thess. 2: 7*.

AND is a past participle signifying *added, one-ed, joined*. It was formerly placed after the words; as, "James, John, David, *and*, (*united to*-gether-*ed*,) go to school." We now place it *before* the last word.

THO, *altho, yet*. "Tho (*admit, allow, the fact*) he slay me, yet (*get, have, know, the fact*) I will trust in him." *Yes* is from the same word as *yet*. It means *get* or *have* my consent to the question asked. *Nay* is the opposite of *yes, ne*-aye, nay, no. The *ayes* and *noes* were called for.

I can pursue this matter no farther. The limits assigned me have been overrun already. What light may have been afforded you in relation to these words, will enable you to discover that they have *meaning* which must be learned before they can be explained correctly; that done, all difficulty is removed.

Interjections deserve no attention. They form no part of language, but may be used by beasts and birds as well as by men. They are indistinct utterances of emotions, which come not within the range of human speech.

END

CPSIA information can be obtained
at www.ICGtesting.com
Printed in the USA
BVHW021410110423
662129BV00010B/672